SPIRITUAL SOLUTIONS

SPIRITUAL SOLUTIONS

Answers to Life's Greatest Challenges

DEEPAK CHOPRA

Harmony Books
New York

Copyright © 2012 by Deepak Chopra

ISBN 978-1-62490-035-8

Printed in the United States of America

Book design by Lauren Dong
Jacket photograph by Jeremiah Sullivan

To the hands that reach out,
and every hand that reaches back

CONTENTS

A PERSONAL NOTE

Ever since my first days as a doctor, forty years ago, people have asked for answers. A medical treatment was what they wanted, but the reassurance and comfort that human contact could bring was just as valuable, perhaps even more so. Unless he's completely burned out, a physician sees himself as a rough-and-ready savior, yanking victims out of danger into a state of safety and well-being.

I'm grateful for my years seeing patients, because I learned the difference between advice and solutions. People who are in trouble are rarely helped by advice. Crises don't wait; something very bad will happen if the right solution isn't found.

I kept the same standard in mind when writing this book. It began with people writing me with troubles on their minds. Their letters were sent from around the world—at one point I was answering questions daily or weekly from India, the United States, and many other locales, mostly through the Internet. Yet in a sense everyone was writing from the same place inside, where confusion and darkness had overwhelmed them. These people were hurt, betrayed, abused, misunderstood, ill, worried, anxious, and at times desperate. Sadly, that is the human condition, almost permanently for some people, but these feelings are always possible for people who are happy and contented—for the moment.

I wanted to give answers that were lasting enough so that when "for the moment" changes, when crisis descends and a challenge must be faced, solid solutions were at hand. I call them spiritual solutions, but the term doesn't mean religious solutions, prayer, or surrender to God. Instead I envision a secular spirituality. This is the only way modern people will ever reconnect with their souls, or, to remove all religious overtones, their "true selves."

What has a crisis done to you personally? Whatever the situation, you drew back, contracted inside, and felt the grip of anxiety. This state of contracted awareness is the enemy of finding a solution. Real solutions to a crisis come from expanded awareness. The inner feeling is no longer tight and fearful. Boundaries give way; fresh ideas have space to grow. If you are able to contact your true self, awareness has no boundaries. From that place, solutions emerge spontaneously, and they work. Often they work like magic, and obstacles that seemed immovable melt away. When that happens, the burden of anxiety and sorrow is lifted completely. Life was never meant to be a struggle. Life was meant to unfold from its source in pure awareness. If this book leaves only one lasting impression, that's the one I'm hoping for.

Deepak Chopra

ONE

WHAT IS A SPIRITUAL SOLUTION?

No one will disagree that life brings challenges, but step back for a moment and ask the deeper question, which is *why*. Why is life so difficult? No matter what advantages you are born with—money, intelligence, an appealing personality, a sunny outlook, or good social connections—none of these provides a magic key to an easy existence. Somehow life manages to bring difficult problems, the causes of untold suffering and struggle. How you meet your challenges makes all the difference between the promise of success and the specter of failure. Is there a reason for this, or is life simply a random series of events that keeps us off balance and barely able to cope?

Spirituality begins with a decisive answer to that question. It says that life isn't random. There is pattern and purpose inside every existence. The reason that challenges arise is simple: to make you more aware of your inner purpose.

If the spiritual answer is true, there should be a spiritual solution to every problem—and there is. The answer doesn't lie at the level of the problem, even though most people focus all their energies at that level. The spiritual solution lies beyond. When you can take your awareness outside the place where struggle is ever-present, two things happen at the same time: your awareness expands, and with that, new answers begin to appear. When awareness expands, events that seem random actually aren't. A larger purpose is trying to unfold through you. When you become aware of that purpose—which is unique for each person—you become like an architect who has been handed the blueprint. Instead of laying bricks and fitting pipes at random, the architect can now proceed with confidence that he knows what the building should look like and how to construct it.

The first step in this process is recognizing what level of awareness you are working from right now. Every time a challenge comes your way, whether it is about relationships, work, personal transitions, or a crisis that demands action, there are three levels of awareness. Become aware of them, and you will take a huge step toward finding a better answer.

LEVEL 1: CONTRACTED AWARENESS

This is the level of the problem, and therefore it immediately grabs your attention. Something has gone wrong. Expectations have turned sour. You face obstacles that don't want to move. As resistance mounts, your situation still doesn't improve. If you examine the level of the problem, the following elements are generally present:

Your desires are thwarted. Something you want is meeting with opposition.

You feel as if every step forward is a battle.

You keep doing more of what never worked in the first place.

There is an underlying anxiety and fear of failure.

Your mind isn't clear. There is confusion and inner conflict.

As frustration mounts, your energy is depleted. You feel more and more exhausted.

You can tell if you are stuck at the level of contracted awareness by one simple test: the more you struggle to get free of a problem, the more you are trapped in it.

LEVEL 2: EXPANDED AWARENESS

This is the level where solutions begin to appear. Your vision extends beyond the conflict, giving you more clarity. For most people this level isn't immediately available, because their first reaction to a crisis is to contract. They become defensive, wary, and fearful. But if you allow yourself to expand, you will find that the following elements enter your awareness:

The need to struggle begins to diminish.

You start to let go.

More people connect with you. You allow them more input.

You approach decisions with confidence.

You meet fear realistically and it starts to lessen.

With clearer vision, you no longer feel confused and conflicted.

You can tell that you have reached this level of awareness when you no longer feel stuck: a process has begun. With greater expansion, unseen forces come to your aid. You move forward according to what you desire from your life.

LEVEL 3: PURE AWARENESS

This is the level where no problems exist. Every challenge is a creative opportunity. You feel completely aligned with the forces of nature. What makes this possible is that awareness can expand without limits. Although it may seem that it takes long experience on the spiritual path to reach pure awareness, the truth is exactly the opposite. At every moment pure awareness is in contact with you, sending creative impulses. All that matters is how open you are to the answers being presented. When you are fully open, the following elements will be present:

There is no struggle.

Desires reach fulfillment spontaneously.

The next thing you want is the best thing that could happen. You benefit yourself and your surroundings.

The outer world reflects what is happening in your inner world.

You feel completely safe. You are at home in the universe.

You view yourself and the world with compassion and understanding.

To be completely established in pure awareness is enlightenment, a state of unity with everything in existence. Ultimately, every life is moving in that direction. Without attaining the final goal, you can tell that you are in contact with pure awareness if you feel truly yourself, in a state of peace and freedom.

Each of these levels brings its own kind of experience. This can be easily seen when there is a sharp contrast or a sudden change. Love at first sight takes a person without warning from contracted awareness to expanded awareness. Instead of relating in the normal social way, suddenly you see immense appeal, even perfection, in one other person. In creative work there is the "Aha!" experience. Instead of wrestling with a blocked imagination, suddenly the answer presents itself, fresh and new. No one doubts that such epiphanies exist. They can be life-changing, as in the so-called peak experience, when reality is flooded with light and a revelation dawns. What people don't see is that expanded awareness should be our normal state, not a moment of extraordinary difference. Making it normal is the whole point of the spiritual life.

Listening to people tell their stories of problems, obstacles, failure, and frustration—an existence trapped in contracted awareness—one sees that reaching a new vision is critical. It is all too easy to get lost in particulars. The difficulties of facing each challenge are often overwhelming. No matter how intensely you feel your situation, which has its own unique difficulties, if you look to the right and left, you will see others who are just as caught up in their situations. Strip away the details, and what remains is a general cause of suffering: lack of awareness. By *lack* I'm not implying personal failure. Unless you are shown how to expand your awareness, you have no choice but to experience the state of contraction.

Just as the body flinches when faced with physical pain, the mind has a reflex that makes it draw back when faced with mental pain. Here again, a moment of sudden contrast makes it easy to experience what contraction feels like. Imagine yourself in any of the following situations:

You are a young mother who has taken your child to the playground. You chat for a moment with another mother, and when you turn around, you can't see your child.

At work you are sitting at your computer when someone casually mentions that there are going to be layoffs, and by the way, the boss wants to see you.

You open your mailbox and find a letter from the Internal Revenue Service.

While driving you approach an intersection when, out of the blue, a car behind you swerves past your car and runs a red light.

You walk into a restaurant and see your spouse sitting with an attractive companion. They are leaning in toward each other, talking in low voices.

It doesn't take much imagination to feel the sudden change of awareness that these situations provoke. Panic, anxiety, anger, and apprehension flood your mind; these are the result of brain changes as the lower brain takes precedent over the higher brain, triggering the release of adrenaline as part of an array of physical responses known as the stress response. Any feeling is both mental and physical. The brain gives a precise representation of what the mind is experiencing, drawing on infinite combinations of electrochemical signals coursing through one hundred billion neurons. A brain researcher can pinpoint with ever-increasing accuracy exactly those regions that produce such changes. What cannot be seen on an MRI is the mental event that incites all these changes, because the mind functions at the invisible level of awareness or consciousness. We can take these two terms as synonyms, but let's explore them a little.

Spirituality deals with your state of awareness. It isn't the same as medicine or psychotherapy. Medicine deals in the physical aspect where bodily changes occur. Psychotherapy deals in a specific difficulty, such as anxiety, depression, or actual mental illness. Spirituality confronts awareness directly; it aims to produce higher consciousness. In our society this is seen as much less real than the other ways of approaching problems. In times of trouble, people cope as best as they can with a swirling confusion of fear, anger, mood swings, and everyday struggle. It doesn't even occur to them to pair the two words *spiritual* and *solution* in the same sentence. This points to a limited vision about what spirituality really is, and what it can do.

If spirituality can change your awareness, nothing is more practical.

Awareness isn't passive. It leads directly to action (or inaction). The way that you perceive a problem will inevitably blend with how you try to solve the problem. We've all been in groups that are asked to accomplish a task, and when the discussion begins, each participant displays aspects of their awareness. Someone seizes the floor, demanding attention. Someone else hangs back silently. Certain voices are cautious and pessimistic, while other voices are the opposite. This play and display of attitudes, emotions, role-playing, and so on comes down to awareness. Every situation lends itself to expanding your awareness. The word *expand* doesn't mean that awareness blows up like a balloon. Instead, we can break down awareness into quite specific areas. When you enter a situation, you respond through the following aspects of your awareness:

Perceptions
Beliefs
Assumptions
Expectations
Feelings

Once you change these aspects—even a few of them—a shift in consciousness occurs. As the first step to reaching a solution, it is critical to break down any problem until you reach the aspects in your awareness that are feeding the problem.

Perceptions: Every situation looks different to different people. Where I see disaster, you may see opportunity. Where you see loss, I may see the lifting of a burden. Perception isn't fixed; it is highly personal. So the key question, when you approach the level of awareness, isn't "How do things look?" but "How do things look *to me*?" Questioning your perception gives you distance from a problem, and with distance comes objectivity. But there is no such thing as total objectivity. We all see the world through tinted glasses, and if you mistake the view for reality, it's just the tint pretending to be clear.

Beliefs: Because they hide beneath the surface, beliefs seem to play a passive role. We all know people who claim to be without prejudice—racial, religious, political, or personal—who act exactly like someone riddled with prejudice. It's easy to repress your beliefs, but it's just as easy not to recognize them. What psychologists call core beliefs can be the hardest to spot in yourself. In an earlier age, for example, it was a core belief that men were superior to women. The topic wasn't even raised for discussion, much less doubt. But when women demanded the vote, and this grew into a broad, vocal feminist movement, men found that their core belief was exposed. How did they react? As if they had been attacked personally, because their beliefs were their identity. "This is me" sits very close in the mind to "this is what I believe." When you react to a challenge by taking it too personally, with defensiveness, anger, and blind stubbornness, some core belief has usually been touched.

Assumptions: Because they shift according to the situation you find yourself in, assumptions are more flexible than beliefs. But they are just as unexamined. If a police cruiser signals you to pull off the road, don't you assume that you have done something wrong and will wind up defending yourself? It is hard to be open-minded enough to allow that the police officer may offer something positive. That's how assumptions work. They leap in to fill a gap of uncertainty. Social encounters are never empty. When you meet a friend for dinner, you bring assumptions about how the evening will go that are unlike the assumptions you bring to a blind date. As with beliefs, if you challenge a person's assumptions, the outcome is likely to be volatile. Although our assumptions shift all the time, we usually don't like to be told that they need to change.

Expectations: What you expect from other people is linked to desire or fear. Positive expectations are ruled by desire, in that you want something and expect it to come to you. We expect to be loved and cared for by our spouses. We expect to be paid for the work we do. Negative expectations are ruled by fear, as when people anticipate worst-case scenarios. Murphy's Law, which says that if anything can go wrong, it will, provides a good example. Because desire and fear lie close to the surface of the mind, your expectations are more active than your beliefs and assumptions. What you believe about your boss is one thing; being told that your salary has been cut is another. Depriving someone of what they expect directly challenges how they live.

Feelings: As much as we try to disguise them, our feelings lie on the surface; other people see them or sense them as soon as they meet us. Therefore we spend a lot of time fighting against feelings that we don't want to have, or against feelings we feel ashamed of and judge negatively. For many people, simply to have a feeling is undesirable. They see themselves as exposed and vulnerable. Being emotional is equated with being out of control (which itself is an undesirable feeling). Being aware that you have feelings is a step toward greater awareness, and then there's the next step, which can be much harder, of accepting your feelings. With acceptance comes responsibility. Owning your own feelings, rather than blaming them on someone else, is the mark of a person who has moved from contracted to expanded awareness.

If you are able to examine your state of awareness, these five elements will emerge. When someone is truly self-aware, you can ask them a direct question about how they feel, what their assumptions are, what they expect from you, and how their core beliefs are being affected. In response you won't get a defensive reaction. You'll be told the truth. Healthy as that sounds, why is it spiritual? Self-awareness isn't the same as praying, believing in miracles, or seeking God's favor. The vision I've sketched in is spiritual because of the third level of awareness, which I've labeled *pure awareness*.

This is the level that religious believers know as the soul or spirit. When you base your life on the reality of the soul, you hold spiritual beliefs. When you go further and take the level of the soul to be the basis of life—the very ground of existence—then spirituality becomes an active principle. The soul is awakened. In reality the soul never sleeps, because pure awareness infuses every thought, feeling, and action. We may disguise this fact from ourselves. One symptom of contracted awareness, in fact, is a complete denial of "higher" reality. This denial is based not on willful blindness but on the absence of experience. A mind blocked by fear, anxiety, anger, resentment, or suffering of any kind isn't able to experience expanded awareness, much less pure awareness.

If the mind worked like a machine, it wouldn't be able to recover from the state of suffering. Like gears worn down by friction, our thoughts would get worse and worse until the day arrived when suffering was completely victorious. For countless people life feels just like that. But the potential to heal is never worn away completely; change and transformation are your birthright, guaranteed not by God, faith, or salvation, but by the indestructible basis of life, which is pure awareness. To be alive is to be caught up in constant change. When we feel stuck, our cells are still processing the basic materials of life continually. Feelings of numbness and depression can make life seem to stop. So can sudden loss and failure. Yet no matter how severe the shock or how stubborn the obstacle, the ground state of existence isn't affected, much less damaged.

In the following pages you will encounter people who feel stuck, numb, frustrated, and stymied. Their stories seem to be unique, as viewed by each of them, but the way forward isn't unique. It consists of addressing their state of awareness. What refuses to move must be shown how to move. That's another reason why the solutions being offered are spiritual: they first involve seeing, waking up, becoming open to new perceptions. The most practical way to reach a solution is spiritually, because you can only change what you first are able to see. No enemy is more insidious than the one you are blind to.

We live in a secular age, and so the view of life I've

just outlined is far from the norm. In fact, it's almost the opposite, because although everyone would agree that buildings must have blueprints, life doesn't. Life is viewed as a series of unpredictable events that we struggle to control. Who will be foreclosed on or lose their job? Which household will be struck with accidents, addiction, divorce? There is seemingly no rationale behind these events. Stuff happens. Obstacles arise of their own accord, or simply by accident. Each of us justifies our contracted awareness by accepting such beliefs, and they run deep. Human nature, we tell ourselves, is filled with negative drives, such as selfishness, aggression, and jealousy. At best we are in partial control of these drives as they rise up inside us. We have no control at all over the negativity in others, and so each day presents us with a struggle against random chance and against people who are out to get what they want, no matter that it causes problems, or even loss, for us. As a beginning to expanded awareness, you need to challenge this worldview even if it is the social norm. Normal isn't the same as true.

The truth is that each of us is entangled in the world we call real. Mind isn't a ghost. It is embedded in the whole situation you find yourself in. To see how that works, first abolish the separation between a thought, the brain cells the thought stimulates, the body's reaction as it receives messages from the brain, and the activity you decide to pursue. All are part of the same continuous process. Even among geneticists, who for decades preached that genes determined almost every aspect of life, there is a new catchphrase: genes are not nouns, they are verbs. Dynamism is universal.

You aren't floating in a mindless environment, either. Your surroundings are being affected by what you say and do. The words "I love you" have an entirely different effect on others than the words "I hate you." An entire society is galvanized by the words "the enemy is attacking." At the most expanded level, the whole planet is influenced by the global exchange of information; you are participating in the global mind by sending an e-mail or joining a social network. What you eat on the run in a fast-food restaurant has implications for the whole biosphere, as environmentalists are at pains to show us.

Spirituality has always begun with wholeness. Lost in a world of specifics, we forget that isolation is a myth. Your life at this moment is an entangled process that involves thoughts, feelings, brain chemicals, the body's responses, information, social interactions, relationships, and the ecology. So when you speak and act, you are causing a ripple that is felt in the flow of life. Yet spirituality goes beyond describing you; it also prescribes the most beneficial way to affect the flow of life.

Because pure awareness lies at the basis of everything, the most powerful way to change your life is to begin with your awareness. When your consciousness changes, your situation will change. Every situation is both visible and invisible. The visible part is what most people fight against, because it's "out there," accessible to the five senses. They are loath to confront the invisible aspect of their situation, because it is "in here" where unseen dangers and fears lurk. In the spiritual vision of life, "in here" and "out there" are entangled with countless threads; the fabric of existence is woven from them.

Two starkly contrasting visions are competing, then, one based on materialism, randomness, and externals; the other based on consciousness, purpose, and the union of inner and outer. Before you can find a solution to the challenge that faces you today, right this minute, you must choose at a deeper level which vision of life you are following. The spiritual view leads to spiritual solutions. The nonspiritual view leads to a host of other solutions. Clearly this is a critical choice because, whether you realize it or not, your life is unfolding according to the choices you have made unconsciously, dictated by your level of awareness.

This sketch of what a spiritual solution can achieve will sound very foreign to many people, however. Most of us avoid confronting ourselves; we are unable to define a vision. Instead, we meet life as it comes, coping as best we can, relying on mistakes from the past, advice from friends and family, and hope. We wind up giving in when we must and clutching at what we think we want. So what would it take to adopt a spiritual vision of your own life? In this book we won't be following the path of conventional religion. Prayer and faith, while not central to the vision that needs to unfold, aren't excluded, however. If you are religious and find comfort and help by turning to God, you are entitled to your version of a spiritual life. But here we will be consulting a much vaster tradition than any of the world's religions, a tradition that embodies the practical wisdom of sages and seers, in both East and West, who have looked deeply at the human condition.

If there is one piece of practical wisdom that the following chapters are about, it is this: Life is constantly recycling itself and evolving at the same time. This must be true of your own life, then. When you can see that all your struggles and frustrations have kept you from joining the flow of evolution, you have the best reason to stop struggling. I am inspired by a famous Indian sage who taught that life is like a river flowing between the two banks of pain and suffering. Everything runs perfectly when we stay in the river, but we insist on grasping at pain and suffering as we pass them, as if the banks offer us safety and shelter.

Life flows from within itself, and seizing on any kind of rigid or fixed position is contrary to life. The more you let go, the more your true self can express its desire to evolve. Once the process is under way, everything changes. Inner and outer worlds reflect each other without confusion or conflict. Because solutions now arise from the level of the soul, they meet no resistance. All your desires lead to the result that is best for you and your surroundings. In the end, happiness is based on reality, and nothing is more real than change and evolution. It is with the hope that everyone can find a way to leap into the river that this book was written.

THE ESSENCE

Every problem is open to a spiritual solution. The solution is found by expanding your awareness, moving beyond the limited vision of the problem. The process begins by recognizing what kind of awareness you are working from, because for every challenge in life there are three levels of awareness.

Level 1: Contracted awareness

This is the level of problems, obstacles, and struggle. Answers are limited. Fear contributes to a sense of confusion and conflict. Efforts to reach a solution meet with frustration. You keep doing more of what didn't work in the first place. If you remain at this level, you will be frustrated and exhausted.

Level 2: Expanded awareness

This is the level where solutions begin to appear. There is less struggle. Obstacles are easier to overcome. Your vision extends beyond the conflict, giving you more clarity. Negative energies are confronted realistically. With greater expansion, unseen forces come to your aid. You move forward according to what you desire from your life.

Level 3: Pure awareness

This is the level where no problems exist. Every challenge is a creative opportunity. You feel completely aligned with the forces of nature. Inner and outer worlds reflect each other without confusion or conflict. Because solutions arise from the level of the true self, they meet no resistance. All your desires lead to the result that is best for you and your surroundings.

As you move from Level 1 to Level 3, life's challenges become what they are meant to be: a step closer to your true self.

TWO

LIFE'S GREATEST
CHALLENGES

RELATIONSHIPS

What opens up a relationship to spiritual solutions? A willingness to expand your awareness while giving space for your partner's awareness to expand at the same time. Thus a spiritual relationship is a mirror in which two people glimpse themselves at the soul level. Spiritual relationship brings the deepest fulfillment. That kind of fulfillment cannot be faked. But what are its components?

As with every aspect of the spiritual path, nothing is fixed. You can try to define the perfect relationship in terms of ideals like unconditional love and complete trust. But in reality there is a process, and even in the best relationships the process has unforeseen twists and turns. In this section you will hear from people caught up in distressing relationships. For them, a process also exists, but it has moved in the wrong direction. When two people who used to love each other find themselves alienated and unhappy, the process that got them there has certain predictable features. Looking at your own marriage or life partnership, do the following apply?

Projection: Your partner makes you angry and frustrated. He claims to be doing nothing to irritate you, much less harm you, but that doesn't change how you feel. The slightest gesture makes you see everything you dislike, all the stubborn traits that never seem to change.

Judgment: You feel that your partner is wrong or bad in some way. You feel a lack of respect, or else a strong sense of blame. You especially condemn the judgment that you feel is being directed your way, which only increases your sense that you are right and she is wrong.

Codependence: Your partner fills in your missing pieces. Together you make a whole person, a united front against the world. But there's a major downside. You feel joined at the hip, and when you disagree, you find it impossible to stand up for yourself like an independent adult. You need your missing piece, because otherwise you would feel a hole inside.

Giving away too much: In order to get along and to show that you are a good wife, you gave away your power. All the major decisions are made by your husband; he has the final say-so. Less often this happens with the husband giving away power to the wife, but in either case you become dependent on someone else for your upkeep, self-respect, appreciation, attention, and ultimately your sense of self-worth.

Grabbing too much: This is the reverse of the preceding point. Instead of becoming dependent, you make your partner dependent. You do this through control. You want to be right; you feel free to blame your partner while always finding an excuse for yourself. You expect to be right. You rarely share or consult. In small ways and large, you make your partner feel that she is less than you.

Relationship isn't an object you can take down from the shelf and polish, or haul off to be repaired. It consists of days, hours, and minutes spent together, and each is lost as soon as it is over. How you cope from minute to minute becomes the sum total of your relationship. Spend those minutes coping badly, and eventually the process leads to deterioration.

The alternative is to cope wisely and well from moment to moment. Skill is required for that. No one is asked to turn a marriage into a pact between two saints. What you need is a connection with a deeper level of yourself, a level from which love and understanding can arise spontaneously. In relationships that are deteriorating, awareness is shallow and contracted, so the impulses that arise spontaneously are anger, resentment, anxiety, boredom, and habitual reflexes. Without blaming yourself or your partner, look upon these as symptoms of contraction that can be changed simply by expanding.

WHEN RELATIONSHIPS WAKE UP

Expanded awareness has its own features. Looking at the best part of your relationship—the times when you feel close and connected to your partner—ask if the following qualities apply.

Evolution: You seek to find your true self and act from that level. At the same time, your partner has the same goal. As much as you want to evolve and grow, you want the same for him.

Equality: You don't feel either superior or inferior. No matter how much your partner may irritate you, at bottom you see another soul. Together you share mutual respect. When arguments arise, you never belittle her. You don't have to force a sense of being equal, with your ego secretly feeling that you are better.

Being real: You expect candor and truth from each other. You realize that illusions are the enemy of happiness. You don't pretend to have feelings that aren't really there. At the same time, you see that negativity is a projection, so you don't indulge in anger and resentment. Being real also means that you feel renewed every day. When each moment is real, there's no need to rely on expectations and rituals to get you through the day.

Intimacy: You take pleasure from being close, and your intimacy is used to understand and to be understood. She doesn't manipulate intimacy to extract more affection and desire. He doesn't back away from intimacy because it frightens him. Closeness isn't a state in which either of you feels exposed and vulnerable. It's your deepest shared truth.

Taking responsibility: You claim what is yours, even when it feels painful. You carry your own personal baggage. There are burdens that the two of you shoulder together, but you aren't seduced into codependency, which forces one person's problems to be carried by two. By realizing that it is "my anger" and "my hurt," not "how angry you made me" and "the way you hurt me," you get past victimization. As justified as it feels to be the victim, there is an underlying lack of responsibility. You are allowing someone else to determine your feelings and decide outcomes that are actually yours to decide.

Surrender through giving: You do not approach surrender as losing. Instead, you ask how much you can give to your partner, and in so doing you attain a higher level of surrender. At this level it is an honor to give because one true self is bowing to another. The feeling is one of love, but it is almost an impersonal love, because you expect nothing in return. Every time you give, you enrich your true self, so the net result is a gain.

If people can be made to see the difference between these two processes, one leading to deterioration between partners, the other leading to shared evolution, the first step toward a spiritual relationship has been taken. But I don't lean on the word *spiritual.* Many couples find that a foreign or even threatening concept. It's more important that the two of them see the value of expanding their awareness. The trick is knowing where to insert the wedge. We all hold tight to our selfish point of view. We know what we want most of the time. We harbor the fantasy that our partners will step aside and give us an easy road to what we want.

With that in mind, it's clear that coaxing each partner to give up or give in is futile. It's tantamount to saying, "I want for you more than I want for myself." No one can honestly say that, especially in a state of contraction. What will work is to address the issue from a different angle, but showing the benefits of expanding one's awareness. You feel more relaxed and less stressed. You give positive emotions space to emerge without fearing that they will be beaten down. Anxiety can come to the surface and be released. Those benefits are selfish, at least at the beginning. Over time, however, expanded awareness creates room for another person. In a relationship that has unfolded for years in a spiritual direction, you naturally find yourself doing the following:

- Relating to your partner emotionally, with trust that your feelings are valued and won't be judged.
- Bonding at a profound level, with complete trust that you are accepted.
- Exploring who you really are and who your partner really is—in other words, uncovering your soul.
- Letting love and intimacy grow without imposing boundaries or letting fear get in the way.
- Following a higher purpose together.
- Raising a generation of children who can be more fulfilled than this generation.

I know this may sound impossible to attain when you look at yourself and your partner today. But a fully spiritual relationship is the natural outcome of a process that you can begin now. The world's wisdom traditions mostly talk in the singular, about how one soul can reach heaven or enlightenment. Yet human beings have always been social, and the growth of the individual—including your growth—occurs in a social setting. Looking around today, one sees countless families where inner growth is wanted, yet it's not an easy subject to talk about.

The spiritual side of life in modern society has been divorced from "real life," which involves endless distractions. We dwell on the everyday things that relationships are about—raising a family, providing the necessities of food and clothing, keeping the peace under one roof. Since relationships are hard at the best of times, trying to achieve a spiritual relationship can seem like a fantasy. But spirituality underlies everything in life. We are souls first and persons second; the world's wisdom traditions repeat this teaching over and over. When you reverse the equation, relating first as persons, troubles are inevitable, because at the personal level we have our own agendas, likes and dislikes, and a host of selfish motives. The true self has no choice but to hide.

EVERYONE NEEDS THE LIGHT

The true self has every reason, though, to come out of hiding. This is how two souls can find each other. Bringing out the spiritual quality in yourself isn't restricted to your primary relationship, however. Every relationship has its own potential that is different and unique. Imagine at this moment that all the people you relate to are like a pie, with each person occupying one slice. Most of the slices will be people who are stable—dependable friends and family who never seem to change. That stability is needed; those relationships make life steady and comforting, even though you may complain that nobody changes or that they can't see how much you have changed. When you go home for the holidays, the table is filled with mostly this kind of person.

Other slices of the pie are different. At least one should be filled with light: this is the person who inspires you, who makes you grow and evolve. Romance isn't always the key. He or she may be the most difficult person you relate to, because your relationship is so open—none of the usual social gestures are wasted between the two of you. I remember a woman who told her partner, "We're not as happy together as we should be." Without hesitation the partner replied, "Maybe our job right now isn't to be happy. It's to be real." At a deeper level, happiness becomes lasting only when it's real. Trying to base your relationship on illusions, however pleasing they are, will fail in the end.

Look for that slice of the relationship pie that is filled with light. *Light* is the essence of the soul. I put the word in italics because light is a metaphor for a range of soul characteristics: love, acceptance, creativity, compassion, nonjudgment, and empathy. Your primary relationship should contain these qualities.

Countless people are not so fortunate, however. No one in their circle of relationships is inspiring; they have no partner in their spiritual journey. The partner they do have may be blocking the way. That's the gist of the problem when people ask about their troubled relationships. The solutions they are seeking don't lie at the level of the problem, however. The solution lies at the level of the true self. When people catch on to that, they can quit blaming their partners, stop feeling victimized, and take responsibility for discovering who they really are. With those keys in hand, spiritual solutions emerge that were not seen before, even when couples say that they have tried everything.

What they haven't tried is the one thing that supports life as a whole: our awareness of who we really are. More than spirituality is at stake. To relate is a journey, hand in hand, of self-exploration. When undertaken mutually, nothing brings greater fulfillment.

||||||||||||||||||||||||||||||||||||||||||||||||||||||||||||||||||||||||||||||||||||||||||||||||||||||||||||||||

The Essence

Relationships run into problems when symptoms of contracted awareness are present, such as

projecting your negativity onto your partner

blaming and judging instead of taking responsibility

using your partner to fill in missing pieces of yourself

giving away your power, becoming dependent

seizing power, trying to control

When these problems arise, the relationship contracts even more, because each partner is contracting. The result is a breakdown of communications. Such relationships develop impasses where both people feel blocked and frustrated.

In a relationship where awareness is expanding, both people evolve together. Instead of projecting, they view the other person as a mirror of themselves. This is the basis of a spiritual relationship, where you can

unfold your true self and relate from that level

see the other person as a soul equal to you

base your happiness on being real, not on illusions and expectations

use intimacy to evolve and grow

get past victimization by taking responsibility for your half of the relationship

ask what you can give before demanding what you can get

HEALTH AND WELL-BEING

Bringing awareness into the field of health is the next and biggest step that needs to be taken. Such a step has been long in coming. Most people define health solely in physical terms, by how good they feel and what they see when they look in the mirror. Prevention focuses on risk factors that are also basically physical: exercise, diet, and stress, with stress being given more lip service than serious attention. Inertia poses a major problem here. Medicine relies on drugs and surgery, which reinforces our fixation on the physical. Even when holistic health programs are proposed, it's common for people simply to exchange pharmaceuticals for herbs, processed food for organic food, and jogging for yoga classes. The shift to a truly holistic approach doesn't occur.

To be holistic, your approach to health must take awareness into account. Awareness is an invisible factor that has powerful long-term effects on body and mind. Consider the following very basic questions:

Do you feel confident that you could break old habits such as lack of exercise, overeating, or subjecting yourself to high stress?

Is impulse control a struggle?

Do you feel unhappy about your weight and body image?

Do you promise yourself to exercise, but take any excuse not to?

Does your enthusiasm for prevention come and go?

How do you feel about the aging process?

Is death a subject you avoid thinking about?

In each of these questions there are two levels. The first has to do with a specific risk factor, such as maintaining your proper weight and getting enough exercise. As we all know by now, decades of public-health campaigns to get people to pay attention to the most basic preventive measures have not prevented an epidemic of obesity, the rise of lifestyle disorders like type 2 diabetes, and a more sedentary way of life—all of these negative trends are moving into lower age groups as well. One reason for such neglect of well-being is our disregard for the second level of well-being, which involves the mind.

Well-being isn't about treating your body right but harboring anxiety and foreboding about how many things might go wrong, or "risk factors." Looking only outside themselves, many people see a world full of risks—germs, toxins, carcinogens, pesticides, food additives, and the list goes on. They ignore the inner world, unless faced with a disorder like depression.

Decades of studies have shown the harmful effects of negative attitudes, stress, loneliness, and emotional repression. If you take a step back, what do all these factors have in common? Contracted awareness. We become more isolated and shut in by mental walls than by the rooms we live in. Let's consider the specifics of how contracted awareness leads to a negative state in the body.

The body's signals are ignored or denied.

Over the past few decades a revolution has occurred in how we perceive the body. What appears to be an object, a thing, is actually a process. Nothing in the body stands still, and life is sustained by something that sounds very abstract: information. Fifty trillion cells are constantly talking to each other, using receptor sites on the cell's outer membrane that capture information from molecules floating past in the bloodstream. Information is democratic. A message from the liver is just as valid as information sent by the brain, and just as intelligent.

When awareness is contracted, the flow of information is hampered, first in the brain, because the brain physically represents the mind. But every cell is eavesdropping on the brain, or receiving instructions directly from it, and within seconds chemical messages deliver good or bad news everywhere in the system. At the most basic level, when you make bad lifestyle choices about diet, exercise, and stress, you are making a holistic decision. You cannot isolate your choices from your body, which bears the repercussions of every negative choice.

The solution: Become more aware and accepting of your body. Stop judging against it. Make connections through sensation and feelings; bring to the surface of our awareness what has been blocked and rejected.

Habits take hold and impulses are hard to control.

Your body has no voice or will of its own. Whatever you choose to do, your body adapts. The range of its adaptability is miraculous. Human beings eat the widest diet of any creature, live in the most varied climates, breathe air at the highest and lowest altitudes, and respond to changes in the environment with the kind of creativity known to no other living thing except, ironically, the very lowest life-forms, viruses and bacteria. Without adaptability, none of us could survive.

Yet we also choose to constrict ourselves and refuse to adapt. This happens through habits. A habit is a fixed process that doesn't change, even when you want it to and the environment demands it. An extreme case would be addictions. An alcoholic receives negative feedback from his body; the people around him ask for change and exhibit extreme distress; the stress of being an addict continues to mount. If an ordinary toxin were involved, such as eating a bad piece of fish or spoiled mayonnaise at a picnic, adaptation would kick in automatically and drastically. The body would discharge the toxin, begin to purify, and reach a renewed state of balance as quickly as possible. But addictions are habits, and they can block every recourse the body has to adapt, until the inevitable breakdown results. In a less extreme way, you are blocking your body through everyday habits like overeating and not exercising, but also through mental habits like worry and Type A control behavior.

The solution: Before acting on a habit, pause. Ask yourself how you feel. Propose to yourself that other choices exist. Can you take another choice? If not, what is stopping you? Habits are broken by stopping the automatic reflex and injecting new questions, from which new choices arise. Fighting against a habit only makes it stronger. Losing the battle is inevitable, and when that happens, self-judgment sets in.

Feedback loops turn negative.

The cells in the body don't engage in a one-way conversation. Their talk is cross-talk, constantly weaving and interconnecting as messages flow through the bloodstream and nervous system. If one cell says, "I'm sick," the others reply, "What can we do about it?" This is the basic mechanism known as a feedback loop. Feedback means that no message goes unanswered, no cry for help unheard.

Unlike society, which gives plenty of negative feedback in the form of criticism, rejection, prejudice, and violence, your body sends only positive feedback. Cells seek to survive, and they can do that only through mutual support. Even pain exists to alert you to areas that need healing.

Yet we have a powerful ability to create negative feedback. Everyone's body has suffered from the conflict and confusion, fear and depression, grief and guilt that run through the mind. Some of this we claim as our right. Human beings take pleasure from crying at sad movies, dwelling on other people's misfortunes, and being shocked by catastrophes around the world. The problem is that we lose control of negative feedback. Depression is uncontrolled sadness; anxiety is fear that persists without being checked. This is the most complex area of contracted awareness, because it can take an entire lifetime to disrupt the body's feedback loops, or it can take a minute. Stress can hit you instantaneously or grind away month after month. Yet there is always the same cause: awareness has drawn into a tight circle, contracting to defend itself from some kind of threat.

The solution: Increase the positive feedback. This can happen internally or externally. Seek the support of friends and counselors. Look inward and learn to release negative energies like fear and anger. Your body wants to restore its weakened or blocked feedback loops. Feedback is information. Whatever brings more information to your mind and body is beneficial.

Imbalances aren't detected until they reach the stage of discomfort or illness.

In the West we tend to see health as a simple fork in the road: either you are sick or you are well. The two choices that face people come down to "I'm okay" or "I have to see a doctor." But the body has many stages of imbalance before disease symptoms appear. These are recognized in Eastern traditional medicine like Ayurveda, where a diagnosis can spot the first signs of imbalance and treat them. The approach is more in keeping with nature, because a patient's sense of discomfort, even a vague feeling that something isn't quite right, still serves as a reliable guide. It has been estimated that over 90 percent of serious illness is first detected by the patient, not by the doctor.

Imbalance covers a host of things, but primarily it means that your body can no longer adapt. It has been forced to accept a state of discomfort, pain, diminished function, or shutdown, depending on how serious the problem is. Observing this at the microscopic level, one would see that the receptor sites of various cells no longer send and receive a steady stream of messages, without which a cell's normal life is impossible. Going out of balance is actually as complex as staying in balance (which is why a cure for cancer, the most drastic behavior in cells, seems more distant and complicated as time goes by), but one major negative factor is awareness. Being well begins by being aware of your body. Nothing is more sensitive, and when awareness is withdrawn or becomes blocked, the body loses part of its ability to know itself, and monitoring breaks down. As precise as medical tests may be, there is no substitute for the self-monitoring that goes on thousands of times per minute inside the mind-body system.

The solution: Break out of the duality of "I'm okay" and "I have to see a doctor." There are many shades of gray, not a simple black or white. Pay attention to our body's subtle signals. Take them seriously; don't withdraw your attention. There is a vast array of hands-on healers, energy workers, and body-oriented therapies that specifically address subtle imbalances before they reach the stage of disease.

Aging creates fear and loss of energy.

If aging were purely physical, it would affect people the same around the world and in different eras of history. But this is far from the case. The breakdown of the body over time has shifted dramatically according to time and place. For every symptom of the aging process once considered normal, there are some individuals who escape the symptom or even reverse it. Rare as they may be, there are people whose memory has improved with age, others who have gotten stronger by taking up exercise in their eighties or nineties, and still others with organs that function like someone ten, twenty, or even thirty years younger.

Physically, despite the huge advances in public health that have extended our life span, the body itself was always capable of longevity. Paleontologists have discovered that Stone Age humans died through exposure to the elements, accidents, and other environmental factors like famine. Without these outside influences, prehistoric people could potentially live as long as we do—witness tribal societies that still live beyond modern civilization and that have a few individuals who survive into their eighties and nineties.

Here is another area where too much emphasis on the physical aspects of aging is shortsighted. The creation of the "new old age" over the past few decades was largely a shift in attitudes and expectations. When the elderly are set aside as useless and worn out, unwanted and isolated, they conform to expectations. Passively awaiting decay and death, their decline fits the model imposed by society. The current generation that is becoming old has rejected those expectations. In one poll of baby boomers, when asked what age they considered to be the start of old age, the average responder said eighty-five! People expect to be healthy and active well beyond three score and ten. By and large this new expectation is turning into reality.

If someone objects, pointing to advances in the medical treatment of the elderly as the chief cause for how long we live, two responses come to mind. First, such advances became possible only after medicine stopped giving up on the elderly. Second, doctors still lag far behind the public in embracing the new old age, as can be shown by the pitifully small number of medical students who choose gerontology as their specialty. Yet without a doubt, whether viewed socially or personally, the aging process is power-fully affected by your state of awareness.

The solution: Become part of the new old age. Re-sources for this are everywhere, so lack of support isn't the issue. What's critical is inertia and your response to it. Becoming isolated and lonely doesn't happen to most people overnight. There are months and years during which passivity and resignation begin to take hold. The period of late middle age (now expanded from fifty-five to seventy, if not beyond) gives you time to construct your own old age, building on the first half of life not for declining years but for renewed inner values that can be expressed in wiser, more fulfilled activity.

Death is the most fearful prospect of all.

The last frontier to be conquered by awareness is death. That is inevitable, given that almost everyone avoids think-ing about death. But at a deeper level, dying would seem to be immune to consciousness. After all, doesn't the mind perish when the body does? What can being aware do about that, the final termination of itself? The answer, of course, is survival after death. The great promise of the afterlife is summarized in Saint Paul's enticing words, "Death, where is thy sting? Grave, where is thy victory?" Almost all world religions echo the same promise, that death doesn't have the last word.

But promises about the future do little to assuage the

fears that visit here and now. If you are afraid to die, your anxiety is probably hidden; you may deny it or refuse to feel that this is an important issue. No medical test has been devised to show how cells are affected by a precise kind of fear, death as opposed to fear of spiders. Yet if you stand back, the most pervasive influence on your whole life begins with how you feel about life and death. Once you define well-being in holistic terms, it is undeniable that being afraid of death must have consequences, such as feeling unsafe in the world, constantly being vigilant about threats, and holding death to be more powerful than life. Only by reversing these consequences can a deep, abiding sense of well-being exist.

The solution: Experience the meaning of transcendence. To transcend is to go beyond an ordinary waking state. You already do that through fantasy, daydreams, visions of the future, imagination, and curiosity about the unknown. Taking the process a step further through meditation, contemplation, and self-reflection, you can expand your awareness to reach an experience of pure awareness. When you are established there, fear of death is replaced by knowing the state of immortality. This is what Saint Paul meant by "dying unto death." You no longer fuel your fears and give them life. Instead, you activate the deepest level of awareness and draw life from it.

Disease and distress need to be healed. Yet over a lifetime, the key to well-being is a person's coping skills. With poor coping skills, you become prey to every accident, setback, or disaster. With strong coping skills, you become resilient in the face of misfortune, and resilience has been shown repeatedly to be present in people who survive to great old age with a sense of fulfillment.

Coping begins in the mind. Your state of awareness is the foundation for all your mental habits and attitudes. From there you develop the behavior of a lifetime. Contracted awareness severely limits your behavior— ultimately that is why people indulge in activities that endanger their health. They can't see a way out because they are trapped inside a very limited vision of possibilities. We will have much more to say about coping skills as these chapters unfold. Most people, sadly, haven't looked at themselves this way. They haven't found the root cause of their dis-ease and distress. The usual recommendations to improve our lifestyles is valid enough, but a higher level of well-being awaits when people tap into the true source of all fulfillment.

SUCCESS

Success is so eagerly pursued that you would suppose it to be well understood. Certain advantages—being born rich, going to the right college, making social and business connections—are generally seen as keys to success. But research undercuts these factors; they do not predict success very well, and some successful people rise to the top without any external advantages. When asked how they became successful, the most common factor that leading businessmen give is luck; they found themselves in the right place at the right time. This implies that if you want to be successful, your best course might be to throw yourself into the hands of random chance.

If there is a better approach to success, we first have to ask what success actually is. A simple definition that cuts through much confusion is this: success is the result of a series of good decisions. Someone who makes the right choices in life is going to reach a much better result than someone who makes bad choices. This holds true despite setbacks and failures along the way. As every successful person attests, their road to achievement was marked with temporary failures, from which they took positive lessons and thus were able to move forward.

What, then, goes into a good decision? Which choices ensure a positive outcome? Now we come to the heart of the mystery, because there is no formula for good choices. Life is dynamic and constantly changing. Tactics that worked last year or last week often don't work anymore because circumstances have changed. Hidden variables come into play. No formula can account for the unknown, and despite our best efforts to analyze what is going on today, there is no getting around the fact that tomorrow is unknown. By itself, the unknown constitutes a mystery. Mysteries are entertaining in fiction; in real life they bring a mixture of anxiety, confusion, and uncertainty.

How you deal with the unknown determines how well you make choices. Bad decisions are the result of applying the past to the present, trying to repeat something that once worked. The worst decisions are made by applying the past so rigidly that you are blind to anything else. We can break down bad decisions into specifics. What we see is that each factor is rooted in contracted awareness. By its very nature, contracted awareness is rigid, defensive, limited in scope, and dependent on the past. The past is known, and when people aren't able to cope with the unknown, they have little choice but to remember the past, using old decisions and habits as their guide—a very fallible guide, as it turns out.

For each factor that holds you back, the solution is to expand your awareness, leaving limitation behind to discover a clearer vision of the problem. Before you read the following list, consider a really bad choice that you made—in relationships, career, finances, or any other critical area—and measure it against the aspects of contracted awareness as applied to decision-making.

LOOKING BACK ON YOUR BAD CHOICES

Did you have limited vision of the problem you faced?

Did you act on impulse, despite your better judgment?

In the back of your mind, were you panicked by fear of making the wrong decision?

How many obstacles came out of the blue, unforeseen in advance?

Did your ego get in the way, making you the victim of false pride?

Were you unwilling to see how much the situation had changed?

Did you focus too much on seeming to be in control? At a deeper level, did you feel out of control?

Did you ignore other people who tried to stop you or change your mind?

Did you overlook a hidden agenda, such as wanting to fail so that you wouldn't have to take full responsibility?

This quiz isn't offered to discourage you. Quite the opposite. Once you bring into view the drawbacks of contracted awareness, the advantage of expanded awareness becomes completely evident. Let's take each factor one at a time.

Limited perspective

In any situation, we never have enough information. Too many variables enter into difficult choices. Since we all make decisions based on less than total knowledge, our limited perspective handicaps us. You can overcome such limitations to a certain extent by learning more about the situation; that is a valuable thing to do, so far as rational solutions go. But imagine choosing your life partner by first reading their past history in complete detail, leaving out not a single day since they were born. Imagine choosing a job by first analyzing every business decision your prospective employer ever made. The more variables you try to take into account, the more ambiguous everything looks.

The solution: Take into account only the information that affects success or failure. No rational model exists for doing this, but at the level of pure awareness, all variables are being computed at the same time. When you expand your awareness, you don't have to sort out a host of confusing factors. The critical factors for making a good choice come to mind from the source, which is within you, not in the external environment.

Impulsiveness

Acting on impulse is emotional, and most bad decisions are impulsive. That part is no mystery. (As one popular adage puts it, "Ready, fire, aim.") Turning decision-making into a rational process is the holy grail of many researchers, who see emotions and personal bias as the enemy of clear-sighted choices. But all such efforts have failed, because emotions are woven into every decision. If you are in a good mood, you are likely to pay too much for an item, buy it on a whim, overestimate how well the future will turn out, and be blinded to the negatives in your situation.

The usual answer to emotional bias is impulse control. Being able to control our impulses is considered a crucial aspect of emotional intelligence. Apparently there are predictors for this from a very early age. In one experiment a child is told that he can have a piece of candy right now, or, if he waits fifteen minutes, he can have two pieces of candy. Only a minor percentage of very young children will take the second option, but those who do are likely to have good impulse control for life. They can tell immediate gratification from delayed gratification and choose the latter. The catch-22 is that the better you are at controlling your impulses, the less you will trust a snap decision, and snap decisions have been shown to be more right than not. Pausing to analyze a decision tends to lead to worse, not better choices.

The solution: Know when to choose now and when to choose later. This isn't something that fits any model. Some impulses lead to good outcomes, others lead to disappointment. At the level of pure awareness impulses are aligned with future outcomes, which means that what you want to do at this very moment will turn out to be right for the future. With expanded awareness, you spontaneously have the right impulse, and if you don't, you instinctively recognize that you need to pause and reconsider.

Fear of failure

Good decision-makers are considered to be bold and fearless. With that in mind, most of us fake it, trying to appear more confident and sure of ourselves than we really feel. The great frauds in history achieved their success by mastering a look of complete self-confidence. But in reality the most momentous decisions are made in the presence of fear and anxiety; a glance at photographs of Lincoln during the Civil War and of Winston Churchill during the Blitz of World War II testifies to their depression, worry, and sorrow.

When fear is an inescapable factor, the real question is how to keep it from destroying your clarity of mind. Someone who is blinded by fear usually feels at the emotional level that a powerful impulse must be followed; they are too afraid to make any other choice. What is more insidious is hidden fear, because you may make the same bad choice as another person who is full of anxiety, yet you will delude yourself into believing that you are not anxious. The paradox here is that we pick leaders who act the most confident, but such leaders are almost guaranteed to make bad decisions due to lack of self-knowledge.

The solution: Find the level in yourself that is actually fearless. This level lies deep within. On the surface the mind is unruly, agitated with the effects of anxiety. A layer below that, the voice of fear continually talks about risks, failure, and worst-case scenarios. At the next layer, other voices make the case for reality, pointing out that fear is convincing but not always right. Only when you can transcend this level do you reach the true self, which views every situation without fear. This is because fear comes from the past, arising from memory of pain. The true self lives in the present; therefore it has no contact with old hurts and wounds. In clarity it can see that risks and bad scenarios exist—these aren't shoved aside or denied— yet in seeing the negatives there is no coloration of fear.

Unforeseen obstacles and setbacks

In the state of contracted awareness, uncertainty is your enemy. You don't fully know how other people are going to behave, and even if you got sworn affidavits with promises to act a certain way, other people don't know how they will behave in the future. Society is in constant flux between things that remain more or less reliable and things that nobody foresees. The so-called black swan theory even holds that history is determined far more by totally surprising, anomalous events than by anything one could have predicted. Individuals seem to feel the same way about their own biographies—as I mentioned above, the most successful among us owe their rise, as they see it, to good luck.

More common than good luck is bad luck or no luck at all. The popularity of Murphy's Law is due to the inevitability of obstacles, though there may not actually be a natural law that if something can go wrong, it will. Blind pessimism is as unrealistic as blind optimism. But a good deal of success involves the ability to cope with unforeseeable setbacks. The best marriages have nothing to do with being perfect, but with coping skills. Everyone has a right to behave erratically, and when this results in conflicts, demanding that other people get back on track and behave predictably doesn't work. Still less does it work to retreat from life because you can't handle the knocks.

The solution: Make uncertainty your ally, not your enemy. All leaps forward depend on reaching into the unknown. Once you see the unknown as the source of creativity, you no longer fear it. Instead, you welcome the fact that life renews itself in unexpected ways. This attitude cannot be applied arbitrarily, however. Unforeseen obstacles reflect a genuine inability to see deeper, and what you cannot see has no power to aid you. It takes expanded awareness to open a channel to the underlying creativity that exists within you.

Ego

If you want others to follow you, make yourself look larger than life. The bigger your ego, the more people will use you as an umbrella. Human nature seems to force those who feel weak to give away even more of their power. But ego is almost as bad in decision-making as fear. One overestimates dangers, while the other won't admit that dangers exist. Under the sway of ego, a person must perform constantly. The one thing the ego is good at is building up an image, and images demand that you put on a show that other people will believe in.

It is exhausting, therefore, to devote so much energy to being a winner, while even more energy must be expended to keeping self-doubt at bay. Anyone who has drawn close to world-famous celebrities senses the unreality that surrounds them, and without reality, there is no basis for good decisions. Ironically, famous people make bad choices because everyone around them says yes to everything. Unbounded freedom is a spiritual state; when the ego pretends to be unbounded, it isn't free but trapped in illusion.

The solution: Act from the true self, where "I" is no longer personal. Instead, the ego of the true self is simply a focus for perception—you have a unique perspective without investing in it. As awareness expands, the ego doesn't die, but changes jobs. The old job was to look after number one; the new job is to look out for the whole situation. You no longer have such a personal stake in the world. Our aim is to benefit yourself while causing no harm to others. Ideally, what you want leads to benefits for everyone. That ideal is only attained at the level of pure awareness, however. At every other level there is duality, and with duality there is a clash between "me" and "you," as we pursue separate self-interests. In expanded awareness you take a closer step toward unifying duality, and as that happens, automatically the conflict between separate selves begins to be resolved.

Unwillingness to change and adapt

Adaptation comes naturally to the body, as we have seen. For a cell to survive, it must respond to the messages that arrive this very minute. Our minds, however, are not comfortable living completely in the moment. Like an inchworm, which keeps half its length on one leaf while reaching the other half to a new leaf, we rely on the past to guide the present. This tactic works in situations where you have to remember a skill; it would be futile, for example, to decide that driving a car must be learned every day. Obviously all knowledge is an accumulation; you build on the past in order to know more in the present.

Where the problem arises is psychologically. The past

is your psychological enemy when it "teaches" you that old hurts, wounds, humiliations, failures, and obstacles are relevant to the present. Most people know the value of being adaptable. Few of us announce at a meeting that we are rigid; we pay lip service to being flexible. Even so, we find ourselves making decisions based on the past, which means that behind every open mind is a mind firmly closed.

A closed mind isn't like a clenched fist, which you can open voluntarily. Something inside tells you that you *must* be closed. This is hard to understand when it isn't affecting you. If you have no racial, ethnic, or religious bigotry, you can't easily comprehend that prejudice feels involuntary. Choice isn't an option. Reality itself is dictated by prejudice, so that the mere sight of a person who comes from a different race, religion, or ethnicity is enmeshed with prejudicial beliefs. In the same way, the fusing of past and present in our minds is occurring unconsciously. Even more insidiously, rigid thinking acts like a defensive wall, turning new ideas into threats for no other reason than that they are new. Giving up your old ways is equated with personal defeat or exposing yourself to an enemy.

The solution: Live from the level of the self that is always present. You cannot will your past to go away. Everyone drags around the burden of memory. Even if you could somehow obliterate your past hurts and failures, it wouldn't be possible to make your amnesia selective. You would also lose the positive aspects of your past, including your emotional education, personal growth, and accumulated knowledge. Memories, for good and ill, are woven into your personal self. Fortunately the true self does not have to be guilty from personal experience. It exists in and of itself; it is the vehicle for pure awareness. The more your awareness expands, the lighter the burden of the past. You find spontaneously that your attention is focused on the present, from which all creative possibilities emerge.

Loss of control

Being in control is a thorny issue. Some people, who psychologically fall into the category of control types, cannot be comfortable with even small amounts of chaos and imperfection. They go too far in the direction of trying to control other people and their surroundings. Another personality type ignores self-control and creates an environment that has almost no boundaries or structures. Both are examples of contracted awareness, each in a different way.

Problems arise when control is either lost or becomes too dominant. Most of us would never make a choice that takes away self-control. For some that means jumping out of an airplane with a parachute, for others that means putting money into a risky venture like oil wells. Risk and control are closely related. When your tolerance for risk is exceeded, what happens? A rational risk becomes a threat instead, and threats make us feel that we will no longer be in control. The more contracted your awareness is, the less reliable is your sense of risk. Thus you feel overly threatened, even by small risks, and you wind up making decisions within tight boundaries. Paradoxically, when you feel really paralyzed is the moment when you are likely to act recklessly; your sudden decision, almost always a bad one, comes about because you want to escape the stress of not making any decision.

The solution: Replace risk with certainty. You have no worries about losing control if you aren't threatened. Once you are certain about yourself, external threats don't exist anymore, because threat is the same as fear, and knowing who you are is a fearless state. Who you are is the true self. Expanded awareness takes you closer to the true self; therefore, fear decreases. When that happens, the issue of control lessens. In its place you experience a state of increased freedom. Reality is allowed to be beyond your control—it always was to begin with—and you feel comfortable joining in.

Opposition from other people

Bad decisions are made when you don't know whom to listen to. The worst decisions are made when you can't even decide whom to trust. There will always be contending voices in the room; total agreement is suspicious whenever it occurs, in fact. Somebody isn't telling the truth. When faced with widely differing opinions, most people choose the ones they already agree with. If you look back on the times you seriously asked for advice, you'll probably discover that what you really wanted was permission to act the way you were going to act anyway. Your motive wasn't to get the best advice; you wanted to feel good about a choice that contained an element of doubt, shame, or guilt.

Contracted awareness is isolating. You are more alone with thoughts and beliefs that are completely private. One effect of being isolated is that other people seem to be far away. You can't reach out to them; sometimes you can't even find a way to communicate with them. The most common example is teenagers, who isolate themselves from their parents as they move from childhood dependency to adult independence. Adolescence is the limbo in between those two states, when no one seems to be on your side except other teenagers. But the isolation of old age resembles being an adolescent in the shared attitude of "no one understands me" (one reason that the very old are sometimes the only refuge for adolescents).

The solution: Understand yourself completely. It is futile to seek to be completely understood by others. No one else has the time to understand where you are coming from except in a fairly superficial way. And even if you spent time with the most empathic person in the world, someone who wanted to understand you down to the last detail, what would be achieved? They would have full knowledge of a person who was constructed from the haphazard circumstances of the past, a rickety, jerry-built collection of old experiences. To truly understand yourself is to know the true self. With that knowledge comes complete trust in yourself. Once you have that, the opinions of others can be seen without threat, and you will have a reliable inner guide that allows you to weigh fairly, without undue personal bias, what contending voices are telling you. Even more important, those other voices will be much less contentious. The secret of operating from expanded awareness is that you are already aligned with the right choice. Others can sense that, which makes them more willing to cooperate.

Hidden personal agendas

Most adults have enough experience to judge when someone else has an agenda. Usually agendas fall into predictable categories. There are givers and takers. There are the ambitious and the timid, the selfish and the selfless. It's crucial to society that we wear our agendas on our sleeves. Otherwise, doubt and suspicion play too great a part. Cooperation collapses when you can't trust other people's motives. At bottom, your own motives are about getting what you want, making your dreams turn into reality.

The snag is that some agendas are hidden, even from the person who has them. We are trapped between "I must" and "I won't." If you have to be liked or to belong, you might not realize how powerfully this "must" affects you, but if you were asked to fire an employee, say no to grown children asking for money, or take an unpopular stand about same-sex marriage, for example, your hidden agenda would make those actions difficult if not impossible. Or consider misers and the habitually stingy. Hidden inside is a fear of lack, and since this fear isn't being confronted, it gets acted out instead. No amount of hoarding or stinginess will make up for the lack, which is psychological, not material. All hidden agendas are psychological, and whatever they are, they will lead to bad decisions because of the contracted state that they are coming from.

The solution: Renounce personal agendas. This involves bringing them to light first. Then you must turn over the rocks and look at what is hiding underneath, which is almost always fear. Fear is the most powerful force contracting anyone's awareness; it demands that we retreat, put up barriers, and defend ourselves. But it becomes far easier to renounce your hidden agendas if you expand your awareness. Bringing the light is always better than fighting the darkness. The true self is the source of light, and you need to discover that the true self is available. Nothing is truer than Jesus' teaching, "You are the light of the world," and yet it seems easier to believe that the light comes from outside ourselves. Hard as it is to claim your darkness, it is almost as hard to claim your light. Fortunately the light is timeless, and even if you turn away from it, messages from your true self never stop being sent.

The ultimate success is to live in the light permanently. Then there are no rigid boundaries, no fears, no limitations. As with everything, the point of our lives is to realize who we are. Once you are established in your own being, the struggles that hinder success melt away. The next time you succeed at anything, even in bringing a smile to a child or appreciating the sun setting over the sea, remind yourself that you have taken a step closer to the real measure of success, the pure awareness that is your source and the source of every happiness you've ever experienced.

||||||||||||||||||||||||||||||||||||||||||||||||||||||||||||||||||||||||||||||||||||||||||||||||||||||||||||||||||||||||

THE ESSENCE

By ordinary measures success is unpredictable. So many factors create it, and some, like timing and opportunity, appear to be random. But what is success? A series of decisions that leads to a positive result. If decision-making can be maximized, success is far more likely.

Decisions based on contracted awareness are unlikely to work out well, because of the following drawbacks:

limited perspective
impulsiveness
fear of failure
unforeseen obstacles and setbacks
ego
unwillingness to change and adapt
loss of control
opposition from other people
hidden personal agendas

With the expansion of awareness, each of those drawbacks begins to lessen, and decisions begin to be supported at a deeper level. In pure awareness all decisions are in line with the universe and the underlying laws that govern both the inner and outer worlds.

PERSONAL GROWTH

Getting closer to your true self has many practical benefits. So far we have focused on the practical side, because it is crucial for spirituality to solve the very real problems that people face. But if you are a parent raising a young child, it would be shortsighted to think of walking, talking, and reading as practical things only. We don't say to a toddler, "Start walking. You may need to run after a bus to get to work." To grow from infancy to childhood, from adolescence to adulthood is valuable in itself. Life unfolds in all its richness as we unfold. The inner and outer worlds mesh into a single process known as living.

Spirituality has its own value, leaving aside all the practical considerations. When you are alone, facing no problems or crises, the situation doesn't call for solutions. Yet your need for spirituality is greater than ever. When you consider what it means simply to exist, the true self beckons. It can tell you who you really are, and nothing is more valuable. That's a grand pronouncement, I know. Anyone can spend a rewarding lifetime ignoring the riddle of "Who am I?" Or, to be more precise, people answer the question by identifying with the everyday self. "I am" can be followed with countless words that apply to ordinary existence. I am my job, my relationships, my family. I am my money and possessions, my status and importance. Into the equation you can add race, ethnicity, politics, and religion. The everyday self is an expanding suitcase crammed with every thought, feeling, memory, and dream you've ever had.

And yet for all that, the true self has not really been touched. The soul, the essence, the source—by whatever name, your deepest identity doesn't unfold without personal growth. Spirituality is voluntary, and in the modern age the vast majority of people opt out. Now that we've covered the practical reasons for not opting out, it's time to see whether the true self is worth seeking for its own worth, not just for what it can accomplish. Lofty ideals are not what we need, either. We need to experience the true self and say, "I choose you over my everyday self." A new kind of self-worth is implied, and a higher kind of love. The bliss of simply existing, if you can experience it, would be chosen by anyone over the ups and downs of ordinary existence, the fragile happiness that is always accompanied by sadness, anxiety, and disappointment.

The everyday self is already flooded with experiences. To arrive at a deeper level requires a process that takes you higher. On a daily basis you must orient yourself to grow in the following areas:

A PATH TO THE TRUE SELF

Maturity—developing into an independent adult
Purpose—finding a reason to be here
Vision—adopting a worldview to live by
"Second attention"—seeing with the eyes of the soul
Transcendence—going beyond the restless mind and
    the five senses
Liberation—becoming free of the "reality illusion"

Your success in these areas depends on your really wanting them to unfold. Personal growth involves the same things that go into learning how to play the piano or to master French cooking: desire, motivation, practice, repetition, and discipline. This is your life you want to transform. A generation ago it was unusual to hear anyone speak about personal growth in these terms. "Finding your true potential" was just emerging as a catchphrase, along with "consciousness raising." Can we say that either one showed people how to reach the goal? Did thousands of aspiring seekers manage to transform themselves? Sadly, the answer was usually no. To find success, you must acquire a trait that protects you from fickleness, illusion, self-indulgence, and loss of motivation. That trait is sobriety. Sobriety is a combination of serious intent and realism. It is an expanded state of awareness that has to be cultivated. If you don't walk the walk, you will remain in a contracted state of the kind known as everyday existence.

Let me apply sobriety, then, to each point on the preceding list.

Maturity

Maturity is a psychological state, not a physical one. It
involves things like emotional balance, self-reliance, mod-
eration, and the possession of foresight. Children aren't
expected to have those things. Adolescents move erratically in their direction. If the journey isn't completed,
you can be fifty while still viewing the world through the
mind of a fifteen-year-old. The demands of everyday life
tend to work against maturity. There are so many distractions and pressures that a person can use as excuses.

You can even say that society now devalues maturity.
Mass media creates the illusion that being young and hip
is much more fun. By comparison, not arriving late at
work or staying after to finish up some paperwork is deadly
dull. But in reality the young are more stressed and anxious
than at any other stage of life. Immaturity begins with the
brightness of youth, but it wanes over the years because
to remain immature is to miss the learning curve that allows you to master your life. *Maturity* doesn't sound like
a spiritual word, but unless the spiritual path is grounded
in mature psychology, it quickly evaporates into wispy
dreams.

Reaching maturity means that you practice the following on a daily basis: Take responsibility for yourself.
Provide the necessaries of life without depending on

others. Stand up for moral values and play your part in keeping society together, beginning with the basic unit of society, your family. Treat others with respect and expect the same in return. Behave fairly and work toward justice in every situation. Learn the value of restraint and self-possession.

Purpose

Almost no one would say that they lead a purposeless life. We don't randomly put one foot ahead of the other. Our lives are formed around short-term and long-term goals. Yet, despite this, at a deeper level countless people do wonder why they are here. They regard with nostalgia a bygone time when being a good Christian, obeying God's laws, fitting into one's social class, or defending your country—among many other kinds of ready-made purposes—was enough to give life meaning. We are left to find our own purpose, one person at a time. But here nostalgia is misplaced. It was always true that life's real purpose was to be found through a personal search.

I've offered the true self as a purpose worth devoting yourself to. Short of that, you can find purpose simply through growing and evolving. Looking to the unseen horizon, your purpose could be as profound as reaching enlightenment. If you are suspicious of being told what your purpose in life should be, that's healthy. The most one should accept is inspiration, which is also the most one can give. The point is to remain aware of your purpose, whatever it is. Everyday existence tends to blur our purpose for being here, swamping it in mundane practical demands. Purpose only survives by paying serious attention to it.

Reaching your purpose means that you practice the following on a daily basis: Do at least one thing that is selfless. Read a passage of scripture, poetry, or inspirational prose that makes you feel uplifted. Share your ideals with someone who feels sympathetic. Without proselytizing, express your purpose for being here; aim to inspire with modesty, not to persuade with force. Help your children to find their purpose; make them see that this is important. Act from your highest values. Don't sink to the level of those who criticize or oppose you.

Vision

When I was young I committed to memory a quotation from the poet Robert Browning that in our grandparents' day was known by almost everyone: "A man's reach should exceed his grasp, or what's a heaven for?" The religious context may have faded away, but it is still necessary to aspire. Our highest aspirations speak to the visionary side of the true self. There are practical aspirations, of course, that are not visionary, such as aspiring to make partner in a law firm or to earn a billion dollars. Material aspirations occupy the front of people's minds, yet in reaching them they don't attain heaven or any other higher ground. The gap between everyday life and the soul remains wide. The yearning for something more isn't ful-filled.

A vision is broader than a purpose. It embraces a world-view, which implies action. You step outside the world-view of those who don't share the same vision. Walking the spiritual path unites you with generations of other visionaries. At the same time, however, you can't ride two horses—the demands of material life are renounced. This isn't the same as giving up on comfort and success. One kind of vision sees such a wide separation between the worldly and the spiritual that materialism is turned into an enemy of the soul. Fortunately, there's another vision that speaks of renunciation, not through physical means but as a new orientation. You put your highest value on spiritual growth while maintaining your everyday life, even engaging in it fully. This is what is meant by being in the world but not of it.

Reaching your vision means that you practice the fol-lowing on a daily basis: Look beyond everyday events to their higher meaning. What is your soul trying to tell you? Question your habits of consumption. Put material success in its proper place. Leave time to be with yourself. Put your values to the test by trusting in the universe or God to take care of you. Appreciate the present moment. See others around you as reflections of your inner reality. Read deeply into the scriptures and literature that express your vision.

"Second Attention"

Being in the world but not of it has to be real, not simply an ideal. We are engulfed by the material world and its demands. How can we put it in its proper place while still earning a living, raising a family, and enjoying some comforts? The answer lies at the level of attention. The things you consider most important draw your attention, and in essence they become your world, your reality. For someone fixated on his career, work becomes his reality because that's what he pays the most attention to. In an age of faith, God became real for the same reason. People didn't necessarily meet God personally or have experiences of the divine but hours of every day were spent either in devotion or doing God's work.

In spiritual terms, this single-minded focus can be called first attention. But there's a different flavor of awareness, so to speak, known as second attention. With second attention you see through the eyes of the soul. To put it succinctly:

First attention: From this level of awareness a person focuses on events in the physical world, pursues individual desires, accepts social values of family, work, and worship, sees the world in linear terms, operating through cause and effect, and accepts the boundaries of time and space.

Second attention: From this level of attention a person transcends the physical world, follows intuition and insight, accepts that the soul is the basis of the self, seeks his source in the timeless, aspires to higher states of consciousness, and trusts in invisible forces that connect the individual with the cosmos.

Second attention connects with the true self and takes you to the essence of reality. This essence can never be destroyed or completely suppressed. The soul awaits its resurrection, not through an apocalyptic end of time but through each individual beginning to wake up.

Reaching second attention means that you practice the following on a daily basis: Listen to the quietest part of yourself, trusting that its messages are true. Put less trust in the physical world, and more on the inner world. Learn to center yourself. Don't make decisions when you are not centered. Don't mistake frantic action for results; results come from a deeper level of being. Bond with at least one other person from the soul. Seek silent communion with yourself and your surroundings. Spend time in the natural world, soaking up its beauty. See past the mask of personality that people wear in public. Express your truth as simply as possible.

Transcendence

The phrase *to transcend* means to go beyond, but how can you really know if you have? In a parable from my childhood, a holy man sits in a cave until the day arrives when he reaches the cherished goal of enlightenment. He cannot wait to tell the good news to the villagers in the valley down below. All the way down the mountain the holy man is in bliss. He's walking through the marketplace on his way to the temple when somebody pokes him accidentally in the ribs.

"Out of my way!" the holy man shouts angrily.

Then he stops, thinks for a second, and turns around to go back to his cave again.

This could be read as a parable about false pride, but it's also about transcending. If you are really established in your true self, the knockabout of the everyday world doesn't shake you. You feel detached, but not because you don't care or because you have zoned out. Spiritual detachment means that you view the world from a timeless place. The place isn't found in a cave on a remote mountaintop. There can be no location for this place except inside you. In practical terms, to transcend involves finding such a place, knowing it, and making it your home.

The traditional methods for transcending lead to second attention. These are meditation, contemplation, and self-reflection. Time has not made these methods outdated, but there's no denying that as modern life becomes more stressful, as the everyday world gets noisier and faster, people have less time for meditation. Even setting aside a few minutes a day somehow slips away and best intentions are forgotten. It would be worrisome if personal growth couldn't be achieved because of external distractions. Personal growth can't be destroyed, however, but only postponed. As long as the true self is real, we will be attracted to it, because deep down each of us has a craving for reality. We don't want to base our lives on illusion. To go beyond, then, isn't about any organized spiritual practice. It's about following your own nature as you seek greater happiness and fulfillment. Spiritual practices have no value except as an aid to get you to your goal.

I fully agree with the teaching that true meditation is twenty-four hours a day. There is great value in setting aside a time-out for sitting silently and experiencing a deeper state inside. But once you open your eyes, refreshed and more centered, what good will it do to throw yourself back into stress and strain? The crucial issue is how to bring inner silence into the real world and make a difference. That's the part that takes twenty-four hours, because it's a full-time occupation to become aware of who you really are. It's also a joyful occupation, and the most fascinating project you could possibly undertake for yourself.

Reaching the transcendent means that you practice the following on a daily basis: Stay centered. Notice the external influences that are making demands on your attention. When carried away by a strong emotion or impulse, take a moment to come back to yourself. Walk away from stressful situations when you can. Don't remain in any situation that makes you so uncomfortable that you aren't yourself. Don't give in to the anxiety of others. Be mindful that you are more than a set of reactions to your environment—you are an expression of the true self, always. In every situation where you feel confused, ask, "What is my role here?" Until you find out, don't act or make decisions. Hang loose until reality begins to reveal itself a little more.

Liberation

In a spiritual vein it is said that creation is the eternal play of opposites—good versus evil, light versus darkness, order versus chaos. Yet the ultimate drama is played out over illusion versus reality. No one wakes up thinking that it's going to be a good day for living in illusion. We assume that our personal reality is real, and therefore it's baffling to realize that everything we see, hear, touch, taste, and smell could be an illusion instead. Modern science has already provided a basis for dissolving the physical world. Every solid object disappears into invisible packets of energy when you delve into the subatomic level, and beyond that, even energy collapses into a construct that has no boundaries in time and space, the so-called wave function.

If you want to lead a life based on reality, the fact that the physical world is an illusion cannot be taken merely as a curious fact, to be ignored as you continue to do what you always do. Just as matter vanishes when you go deep enough, so do time and space. They spring from the quantum vacuum, a void that appears to contain nothing, but that in actuality serves as the origin of every event since the Big Bang, along with infinite possibilities that have not yet emerged in the cosmos. In the world's spiritual traditions, the state of infinite possibilities is not a far-away, unimaginable condition but the very ground state of existence.

The true self liberates you because it brings you out of limitation, grounding you in a reality that is timeless, without boundaries, and infinite in its possibilities. The whole issue of illusion versus reality must become personal if you want to be free (we'll discuss this in more detail in the final section of this book). The first step is a moment of disillusion. You stand back and admit that you do not really know the basis of your existence. By surrendering to what you don't know, you can allow knowledge to flow in. That's the true meaning of surrender. You are like a prisoner who stares at four narrow walls lit by a small window high up. The prisoner faces reality if he admits that he is in prison.

But what if he doesn't? What if he thinks that his cell is the whole world? Then his notion of freedom would be insane. The same conclusion applies to each of us in our limited lives, but we don't label ourselves insane. After all, everyone we know accepts being imprisoned as normal. Only a small, strange band of saints, sages, and visionaries sends up a loud cry for freedom. When you hear that cry, the beginning of transformation is at hand. Liberation is real because the timeless is real, more real than anything your five senses detect.

Reaching liberation means that you practice the following on a daily basis: See beyond your limited situation. Take as your first principle that you are a child of the universe. Dwell on those moments when you feel free, exhilarated, unbounded. Tell yourself that you have touched what is truly real. Seek love as your birthright, along with bliss and creativity. Dedicate yourself to exploring the unknown. Know that there is something infinitely precious beyond the reach of the five senses.

Someone might protest, "How can I ever change? This is all so overwhelming. There's too much to do." I sympathize. When you lay out the particulars of personal growth, the panorama looks vast. It's for good reason that the Indian tradition speaks of enlightenment as being like a gold palace, which brings bliss and freedom, while dismantling your old reality is like tearing down a hut, which brings panic and dismay as the walls collapse around you. To state the case without metaphors, when you look around, the world seems real. And so it is, but it's a reality without the true self. When you reach the end of the journey, you look around, and once more the world looks real. Only this time you are fully awake, established in the true self. In between these two poles, life is confusing. There are days when you get it. Events unfold as if someone upstairs were watching over you (in fact, you are watching over yourself). There are other days when the spiritual life vanishes like a dream, and you are mired in the same hard slog as everyone else.

What keeps you going? Think of children and how they develop. Through good days and bad, through smiles and tears, a hidden reality is unfolding. The surface of life doesn't tell the real tale of neural pathways, genes, and hormones as they come together in concert to make a new person out of the unformed material we were given at birth. Nature protects our growth. Spiritual growth is liberated from that kind of determinism. Destiny is no longer biology. You have to make a choice to evolve, but that, too, is natural. If evolution is going to shift from the body to the mind, then the mind must enter into the decisions that determine how you evolve. Despite life's ups and downs, the project of evolving isn't complex. All you need to ask is one question: *If I choose X, will it add to my evolution or take away from it?*

You may not like asking that question. There are plenty of times when immediate pleasure or recklessly giving in to an impulse is more attractive. You may not like the answer you get, either. Evolution is usually unselfish, and we are all conditioned to look out for number one, either from greed or from desperation. None of these obstacles matter; nor does resistance, disappointment, or backsliding. As long as you can ask that one question—*If I choose X, will it add to my evolution or take away from it?*—you are stepping toward freedom. The great wisdom teachers would declare that failure is impossible, in fact. Simply to ask yourself if you are evolving is evolution itself.

THE ESSENCE

Your true self is the real you, but how can this be experienced? The everyday self is already flooded with experiences. To arrive at a deeper level requires a process. On a daily basis you orient yourself to grow in the following areas:

Maturity—developing into an independent adult
Purpose—finding a reason to be here
Vision—adopting a worldview to live by

"Second attention"—seeing with the eyes of the soul

Transcendence—going beyond the restless mind and
the five senses

Liberation—becoming free of boundaries and
attachments

When all these aspects of your true self begin to grow,
they combine toward one goal: breaking down the "reality
illusion" that keeps you from knowing who you really are.
The end of the reality illusion marks the stage of evolution
known as enlightenment.

THREE

DEAR DEEPAK:
ONE TO ONE

Nothing can replace connecting with people grappling with problems in real life. This book grew out of letters written from around the world, and in this section you'll find a selection of them.

Each writer felt troubled, and most felt unable to solve their dilemmas. The aim with my answers was always to open up a fresh perspective, following the principle that the level of the answer is never the level of the problem.

Feeling Unlovable

I've worked hard to change my life for the better, but I continually deal with negative thinking even when things are actually okay. I get into a space of hating myself and thinking that the love people show me is a fiction. I've conquered a lot in my life, but this pattern is affecting my relationships and how I treat myself. How do I change?

—Evelyn, 43, Toronto

What you are talking about is past conditioning, and it affects us all. Whether you call these influences from the past emotional debt or karma, they function the same way. A new experience enters the mind, but instead of being evaluated for itself, the experience is shunted down a well-worn track. This happens so automatically that we don't have time to intervene. Let's say that past conditioning tells you that you are unlovable. Then when someone says "I love you," you react not to those words but to old doubt, insecurity, and negative experiences with love. The new gets obliterated by the old.

If this is the case, how do we get rid of old conditioning? I often approach the problem through the concept of "stickiness." Some old memories are stickier than others. They cling to us and we can't shake them loose. What makes an experience from the past so sticky? If we can break it down, perhaps each aspect will be easier to deal with one piece at a time. Let's stay with feeling unlovable.

Feeling that you are unlovable usually has the following aspects that make it stick to you:

1. Someone in authority, usually a parent, told you that you were unlovable.

Solution: Realize that this person no longer has authority over you, and you are not the child you once were. Ask if this person was in fact the one who was unlovable. Ask if this person could even give love to the most lovable child in the world. If the information you took to be true is actually highly unreliable, why accept it?

2. Being loved was scary in the past.

Solution: Find safe ways to get over the scariness. One way is to help a needy child. You will find yourself loved in an innocent, grateful way that is very safe. Examine what the scariest part of being loved is for you. Is it rejection? A sense that the real you will be exposed and found unworthy? Don't evade these questions, but examine them, first alone and then with a confidant you trust.

3. Love seems far away and long ago.

Solution: Get to the bottom of regret. Regret is a two-edged sword. It has a kind of nostalgic side, a sweet melancholy that feels protective, but it also has a self-defeating side. It tells you that it is never better to have loved and lost. The experience is painful, and when it turns into an excuse to never love again, regret is a mask for fear. Look at your regrets and then renounce them.

4. Love is tied in with negative emotions.

Solution: Realize that emotion is the strongest glue of all. The things we feel strongest about turn into indelible memories. The way to unstick the memory is to work through the emotion. Bad feelings have to be faced. The trick is not to relive them again. To avoid that may take a good counselor or therapist. But know in advance that there's a big difference between a negative feeling you are hiding and one that is leaving you. Give yourself permission to experience what letting go really feels like.

5. Memories have turned into beliefs.

Solution: Stop generalizing. We all turn our worst experiences into rules about life, but such beliefs are false. Just because a schoolyard bully made your life miserable at age ten doesn't mean that the world is out to get you. The worst breakup in the world doesn't mean you are unlovable. Look at your most negative beliefs and untangle them from bad experiences that no longer exist. As you yourself point out, your present life is good; it's your interpretation of it, based on flawed beliefs, that is undermining you.

6. Electric fences can't be touched.

Solution: When a feeling is so painful that you can't bear to look at it, it acts like an electric fence. The very prospect of touching it, which is the real solution to any feeling, becomes a deterrent. You will find that touching the fence is possible, but it has to be worked up to. If you feel shame inside, or if a parent abused you or otherwise betrayed your trust, then love becomes an electric fence. What should be a joyful feeling has been merged with pain. The two must be untangled before you can touch upon love without hurt. If you know that you are suffering in this way, professional help is definitely called for.

7. *"I have to be this way."*

Solution: The voice that tells us that we can't change is one that countless people believe. They choose inertia, yet think it was forced upon them. The answer is to reclaim your freedom of choice. Look at the thing that simply cannot be changed. Sit down and approach this as not *your* problem, but as one belonging to a friend. Write this friend a letter containing all the best, most objective advice you can devise. Tell your friend that she has a choice to change, always, and then give specific steps to bring about this change. If you find that you draw a blank, consult a good book about change and adopt the advice given there.

When you approach old conditioning through these steps, getting free of the past becomes viable. It's never easy to delve deep into oneself, where the old traumas and wounds lie in hiding, but if you approach the project rationally and patiently, it will be possible to bring light and dispel the darkness.

Good Works, No Reward

I am a smart, educated woman with a successful career in fundraising. I have raised millions of dollars for elected officials, education organizations, and the arts. However, I do not have a penny to show for it. I face five years of unfiled taxes with no savings, and last year I lost my home to foreclosure. What is my shadow trying to teach me?

—*Rachel, 41, Fort Lauderdale, Florida*

Thank you for such an honest question, and I congratulate you on realizing that your shadow—the darkest aspect of the unconscious mind—is trying to tell you something. You haven't fallen back on blaming others or feeling victimized by fate and bad luck. (Of course, all of these ingredients could be circulating inside at a deeper level.)

As you state the case, you are a natural helper. You have been successful at giving others more well-being while depriving yourself. Why would anyone do such a thing, since, for most people, charity begins at home? There are several possible answers, and I'd like you to examine each one carefully to see if it applies.

- You think self-sacrifice is a form of virtue.
- You want your good works to be spontaneously rewarded because they prove how good you are.
- You view charity work as a kind of martyrdom, and that appeals to you.

- By helping others, you avoided looking at yourself.
- You hoped that your good works would solve your own unfaced problems.
- You knew you were getting into trouble but didn't want to face reality.
- Some unforeseen things happened that were beyond your control.

Depending on which of these statements holds true for you, the message will be different. Yet I can venture a generalization and say that the shadow always does the same thing: it keeps you in a fog of illusion. The list I've just given you is really a list of foggy illusions. The shadow has brought to your doorstep the very thing you most feared. By not facing it but choosing to remain in a fog, you have wound up facing it anyway, and probably in a more desperate context. Only when you bring awareness to your situation and face reality will the healthier, more positive aspects of consciousness come to your aid. These exist, I assure you, despite your present bad situation. Everything you can do to make facing reality more desirable, as a way of life, than self-delusion will be a step in the right direction.

Why Am I Here? What's It All About?

Are we born with a spiritual or divine assignment to fulfill on Earth, and if we are, what happens if we don't fulfill it? What is the difference between a spiritual assignment and a purpose or calling? Can one miss a divine connection, and is that it, or do you get another chance somewhere down the line? Is it normal for a person to have more than one dream?

—Aphrodite, 49, Dallas, Texas

You ask not one question but a twisted tangle, and the thread that runs through this tangle is self-doubt. I imagine you find it hard to find a purpose or to feel engaged. You easily drift away into speculation, and by seeing so many sides to every question, the urgency to do anything evaporates. My basic issue, then, is whether you really want an answer. Are you happier spinning out unanswered questions? Some people are. They prefer fantasy, daydreams, and passivity to staking a claim to real life.

As to the specifics of your question, some spiritual teachers declare that we make a soul bargain before we enter a new incarnation, and fulfilling this bargain becomes the focus of our existence. How is such a purpose discovered? By following your natural inclinations. What is right for you won't be hidden if you are connected to yourself and willing to follow where your desires lead you.

But many people find this a hazy and untrustworthy notion. They flirt with having a unique purpose, while at the same time maintaining a safe existence based on conventional norms. No higher power is going to punish you for this. A soul bargain, if such a concept is valid, is nothing more than an agreement with yourself. Can there be more than one dream? Certainly. The real question to ask is if you have disappointed yourself. Does anything else really matter? If you aren't disappointed, then you are following the right path. If you are disappointed, you face a choice. You can continue to live with your disappointment or you can retrace your steps and pick up your heart's desire where you abandoned it.

I know what I would do in such a situation, and I think you do, too.

Carrying a Heavy Burden

Seventeen years ago, I gave birth to a beautiful daughter born with birth defects. I thought that I had moved on and made peace, but I am afraid that I just buried my pain. I was preoccupied with raising three young kids and keeping up with the doctor visits, therapists, and household duties. Now it feels that each missed milestone is unbearable. I used to be resilient, but I just can't bounce back. I am overweight, my house is a mess, and I can't seem to claw my way out.

—*Christa, 44, Syracuse, New York*

There are solutions to your situation, but you must take them seriously and begin to act. The basic tenet I have to offer is that happiness is built up by making your day happy. You have to think long term about your daughter, but you have made this an obsession. Situations as tough as the one you describe must be disentangled here and now. Here are the steps that will make your days increasingly happy.

Step 1. Clean your house and straighten out the external mess. There's no reason to be depressed by having to look at chaos every day. If you feel inclined to being miserable, attack a chore. You need to be moving physically in a positive way.

Step 2. Set aside one hour each day to do something that you enjoy a great deal. Don't skip this hour. Don't fill it in with eating, cooking, or television. What you want is an inner sense of creative satisfaction.

Step 3. Spend at least one hour and preferably two hours every day connecting with other parents of disabled children. Seek a support group, telephone connections, e-mails, and online blogs. Research has shown that personal connection of this kind is a key factor in becoming happy. I would make room for connecting with friends and family—that's also beneficial—but in your case it's key to get sympathy and support from others who, like you, are walking the walk.

Step 4. If therapy is making your daughter worse, pull her out and go elsewhere. A trained therapist can help her. Don't stop short in this area. Be patient but keep going.

Step 5. Sit down and address your hopelessness. I am not speaking of the psychological reasons so much as the practical ones. You seem hopeless primarily because you feel that your daughter is doomed. That is a negative belief and a projection, not reality. Nobody can foresee the future. By believing that your daughter can have a good future, you will find that opportunities will unfold to bring it about. Before that can happen, however, you need to sit down and write out the ten things that make you feel hopeless about your daughter, followed by the realistic steps you can take to avoid those outcomes.

You are carrying a burden that doesn't need to be so obsessive, dark, and difficult. The key may be to find other parents who have gotten out of their dark place, and in so doing you will get out of yours. Your old self isn't dead; it's just hidden under blankets of sadness and helplessness that you can clear away.

Ask More from Life

I have been searching my whole life for my purpose, only to discover that maybe I don't have one. I am even more questioning since I'm unemployed after working many years with the same company. Does each life have a specific purpose? (Don't worry; I don't expect a great revelation in your answer. You are only human.)

—*Deborah, 61, Pittsburgh, Pennsylvania*

I don't know if this will come as a revelation, but your purpose in life is to quit asking for so little. Working for the same company has dulled your excitement and sense of expectation. I'm sure you had those things once, and they can be revived. The secret is to peek under the blanket. What have you hidden under there? I have in mind all the tiny seeds of dreams and desires that got tucked away for a rainy day.

Write these words in lipstick on your mirror: "The rainy day has arrived." You are at a time in your life where fulfillment counts for everything. With two or three decades still ahead of you, there's more than enough time to sprout some of those seeds. I can't tell you what they are, but I know they exist.

Choosing Between Right and Wrong

Who decides something is moral or immoral? What I consider immoral might be perfectly fine with someone else.

—*Gurpreet, 26, India*

It is not hard to see that your question is incomplete. You are facing a particular moral dilemma. You want to know if your choice is immoral and might be condemned by others. Yet you are already guilty enough that you don't want to tell us what the problem really is. Because countless people find themselves in similar predicaments, let me address how to make moral decisions. I feel that this will be more practical than addressing the cosmic question of what makes things moral (good) or immoral (bad).

In a dualistic world, we are told that the play of light and shadow, good and evil, has roots in the eternal. Creation is set up that way, and we are caught up in the play of opposites. If this explanation, which is essentially religious, has a strong hold upon you, then decisions about right and wrong become easier. You can consult the religious system you adhere to, and follow its precepts about how to live the life of a good person.

On the other hand, you may be caught between desire and conscience. You want to do something, yet you feel guilty or ashamed about what you want. A married person who is tempted to cheat goes through such a struggle. Society says that the desire or temptation is bad and should be resisted, while remaining faithful in marriage is good and should be honored. If you value the judgment of society and want to be seen as respectable, the right choice is clear. Most of everyday life consists of balancing desire and conscience—doing the right thing even when you don't completely feel like it. People who live successfully within the social system have learned impulse control. My only comment is that choosing to be respectable is itself a desire, so the choice is not between good and bad. Quite often the choice is between a fleeting impulse and a more mature desire. The condemnation of desire doesn't make someone moral; it just makes them out of touch with desire.

Finally, I would say that with even more maturity, a

person can evolve to the point where decisions about right and wrong become less judgmental. You find that your inner guide can make such choices without fearing social condemnation. You are no longer so attached to rigid rules and dictates. A doctor who must decide whether to assist a patient to die, in the interest of relieving the pain of a fatal illness, will make that decision based on very personal considerations. There is no fixed answer in advance. Society rejects too much freedom of choice. It is easy for someone to excuse their own bad actions by saying, "What is immoral for others is moral for me." That is self-centered rationalizing, not higher evolution. Yet higher evolution exists, and the world's scriptures tell us that in higher consciousness unity prevails over duality. In other words, instead of condemning evil, a person becomes compassionate toward the wrongdoer and practices forgiveness.

I hope these comments are of some help to you.

Kissing Lessons

I picked up the morning newspaper and found an article on different types of kisses. I hid the paper, fearing that my teenage daughter would read it. Did I do the right thing?

—*Shipra, 46, Dehradun, India*

Keep up the good fight. But know this: If keeping unsuitable printed matter away from young people helped them to walk the right path, publishers would go out of business overnight and the world would still be full of teenagers learning how to kiss. Such is human nature.

Taking Charge of Your Life?

Every day I wake up and promise myself that I'm going to live each day to the fullest and not let my emotions or fears hold me back. I'm going to do that thing that I've been putting off, talk about that issue that has been eating away at me with someone, but after bathing and having my breakfast, I lose my nerve. How do I take charge of my life? How do I stop letting fear get the best of me?

—*Marissa, 19, Botswana, South Africa*

When you say "take charge," you are actually defining the obstacle, not the solution. You are setting up the situation so that it takes effort, will, and fortitude to face life's challenges. As long as you confront a daunting obstacle, quite naturally you will take the course of least resistance. The same setup causes millions of people to overeat, for example, because the alternative is too much effort and trouble. Let's put it off until tomorrow. Meanwhile, pass the chocolate cake.

The solution is to keep making it easier to overcome your resistance. If you could face life's challenges, including your fears, with enthusiasm and energy, that would be ideal. You can't achieve the ideal overnight, but you don't have to. Taking positive steps every day is good enough—better than good enough, really, since most of the resistance we encounter inside comes down to old, outworn habits and inertia. Getting past them is more than half the battle. Here are the steps I have in mind.

Step 1. Look at your procrastination. This is an ingrained habit, but why do you cling to it? Because putting off unpleasant things offers itself as a kind of "solution." It's a feeble solution, on the order of "out of sight, out of mind." But the things we put off aren't really out of our minds. Just below the surface they nag at us and make it impossible to be carefree. Sit down and absorb this concept: procrastination is a false friend. Recall all the times in the past when you faced up to a problem and felt good about yourself. Realize that procrastination never feels good. It is based on wishful thinking, that somehow a problem will solve itself. Believe me, any outcome is better than waiting, because the longer you wait, the more your mind will invent worst-case scenarios.

Step 2. Make a list for how to have a good day. First thing in the morning, write down what you are going to eat, the errands you are going to run, the bills you are going to pay. Don't extend this list beyond one day. Include on it at least one thing you want to accomplish that you have been putting off. As you write, check in on your comfort level. Everything on your list should lead to the same result: you will feel good today.

Step 3. Carry out your list, and as you accomplish each thing, check it off. At that moment, see how you feel. If you wind up feeling tired or bored or anything negative, revise your list. The whole point of the list is to build yourself a new comfort zone, one based on fulfillment and accomplishment. These things can only come about when your life is manageable. Nobody is happy when their day is overwhelming and exhausting. When you get into the grip of procrastination, all the things left undone build up until they truly are overwhelming, yet you can't break out of this vicious circle until you begin to act. Once you learn that you can face a few challenges while still feeling good—in fact, facing them makes you feel even better— then that little voice inside that says, "Put it off; one more day won't hurt anybody," will begin to lose its power to persuade you.

Spiritually Stuck

I have been on a spiritual journey for twenty years and have studied many different approaches. I work at encouraging others to trust in the process, but right now I'm in a financial situation of lack and limitation. I know that there is a spiritual lesson here about trust. But I seem to be stuck and cannot break through.

—*Bernice, 63, Raleigh-Durham, North Carolina*

To begin with, this isn't a case of now or never. By putting pressure on yourself, you are closing off the channels of help and support. I am not being mystical here. Spirituality is about consciousness, and whatever expands consciousness serves to open up subtler realms of experience. At the same time, whatever closes down your awareness and contracts it with fear cannot be considered spiritual. In other words, I detect that you would like to love and trust, yet at the same time a powerful instinct leads you to be anxious and apprehensive. This is the two-way glass you describe in your letter.

If I may, let me talk about "spiritual materialism," because I think it applies to many of us. When we ask God or Spirit to bring us money—usually disguised in the more polite term, abundance—then spirituality descends to the level of getting and spending. From the ego level springs all the insecurity that makes us want to protect ourselves with money, status, possessions, and various worldly things. Certainly providing for yourself is important. It's not that God gives more if you live up to certain standards and gives less if you don't. There is no all-seeing judge above the clouds, keeping tabs on who is naughty and nice. To think in those terms is spiritual materialism.

Why do so many people fall into such thinking? The reasons are not hard to find. We live in a material society, and in America it's particularly harsh because there are few if any safety nets. The hidden side of prosperity and success is the fear that if you fall, nobody will catch you. Moreover, we have been filled with simplistic promises about God saving the poor and weak, like an all-purpose rescue mission. And even though countless prayers go unanswered, people cling to wishful thinking. Told as children that God is looking out for them, they see no alternative but to cling to those beliefs.

That is why, in the end, spirituality is a path that every person must walk. The path only leads inward. It doesn't lead to a teller's window where you exchange lack for abundance. I know that I'm throwing a splash of cold water, but when you stop believing in illusions, there's space for reality. The reality is far greater than money or anything material. As you walk the path, you discover your true self, and as that discovery deepens, peace and security become permanent aspects of yourself. Fear has been disguising your true self. Ego has been enticing you to measure your progress by externals.

Yet what really matters is a process that allows you to switch your allegiance away from spiritual materialism while finding a new allegiance in being awake. With expanded awareness you find that life has more to offer than you ever knew about. I can't predict whether anyone will become rich or poor. But you are right to trust in the process of life, so long as that doesn't turn into fatalism. There is a right and good place for you in this world; it opens to you when your awareness is open enough to perceive it.

A Domineering Mother

I am my mother's only child and had to move her in with me when she became seriously ill six years ago. She is much better now, fortunately, but still here. Mom has always been negative toward me when it comes to my choices in life. We have never had an adult mother-daughter relationship built on respect. I used to stand up to her bullying, but nothing ever changed. Now I've surrendered to keep peace. She may have loved me as a child, but I don't think Mom loves me as an adult. What can I do?

—*Terry, 40, Charleston, South Carolina*

Don't feel alone with this problem; many grown daughters are walking in your shoes. You have two problems to solve, actually, not one, and the beginning of a solution is to untangle them:

Problem No.1: psychological dependence on your mother

Problem No. 2: your mother's narcissism and self-centeredness

These two issues are entangled, which makes them more difficult to deal with, but the second is the easiest. Your mother is selfish and self-centered. Insofar as she cares about you, it's only as a reflection of herself. The first thing she thinks about is "How does this situation make me look?" If you choose a man, a job, or a pair of shoes, she doesn't care how it affects you. She cares about her own image and egotistical sense of self.

You cannot solve this issue, because it's not yours to solve. As long as you keep giving in to your mother, she has "solved" her narcissism by keeping it under wraps and denying that it's a problem. If she were the slightest bit unselfish, she would see the bad effect she is having; she would empathize with your feelings. She would thank you for nursing her and quickly move on. She does none of these things. Therefore, you really don't have to consider her feelings when it comes to repairing your own life.

The first problem, your dependency—or, to use modern jargon, codependency—is more difficult. It's one thing to be a fly caught in the web struggling to break free. It's quite another if you're a dog or cat who claims to be caught in a web. They can easily break free if they want to. So the big question is, why don't you want to be free of your mother, given that a real desire to be free would immediately lead to action? When you have a rock in your shoe, you don't put up with it unless you happen either to like pain or want to suffer as a martyr.

Dependency is rooted in a child's need for love. A healthy child grows out of dependency and realizes that "I am lovable." A dependent child remains attached and says, "I am only lovable if Mommy gives me love. Otherwise, I am not." Until this root cause is resolved, dependency will spread to other areas. Approval, success, the feeling of being safe, personal accomplishment, and so on, become based upon what others say about you, rather than securely grounded in knowledge of your own self-worth.

I think it would help you to read about codependency. Once you feel that you see yourself realistically, find a group that deals in codependency issues. You will need help extricating yourself. Your mother is a powerful personality. She knows how to keep her hooks in you. Remember, when you break free, you will be able to love her more honestly. That is better than feeling trapped and pretending to love your tormentor.

Parenting an Addict

How am I to emotionally deal with having an adult son who is drug dependent? When he is using or his life is in chaos, I don't know how to keep his situation from occupying my mind 24/7—there's a feeling of doom surrounding me. Can I deal with this from a spiritual standpoint? How does a parent let go of the pain and anxiety I feel?
—*Bernadette, 61, Milwaukee*

It would take days to go into detail about parent-child relationships, but you are asking about an issue we can isolate: the guilt, anxiety, and frustration of not being able to help. In spiritual terms, this is about attachment. You identify with someone who is separate from yourself. You all but lose the boundary between yourself and your son. Attachment makes you obsess over your son's chaotic life. It makes his pain feel like yours.

Please see that I am not criticizing the loving empathy that connects a mother and son. You can get beyond crippling attachment through a process that involves the following steps:

1. See that attachment isn't positive. It helps no one. The most effective therapists tend to be unattached, even detached. It gives them clarity and objectivity. It allows their skills to be used most effectively.

2. See that your attachment is harming you. As close as you feel toward your children, the life that is closest to you is your own. Sacrificing a good part of it to suffering is destructive. You must value yourself enough to want a good life for yourself. From this goodness you will offer more help to those in need, not less.

3. Reject false hope, wishful thinking, and the constant recurrence of "solutions" that never work and that your children reject anyway. If they say no, be an adult and accept that *no* means *no*.

4. Heal your wounds. Most addicts have lost the ability to care about those around them. They are in the habit of hurting, rejecting, betraying, keeping secrets, and breaking faith. The disease works that way. But all that negative behavior has hurt you. Don't let parental guilt turn you into a punching bag or a rug to trample over. Heal yourself where you hurt.

5. Fulfill your primary relationship. You don't mention your husband, but if you are still married, repair your bridges with him. This is not a path to walk alone. Realize that your children are not your primary relationship. If they are all you have, that still doesn't make them your primary relationship, because they aren't relating to you at all. Find someone to relate to who cares for you. They certainly don't.

6. Find a vision to follow. Right now, your vision is an illusion. It is fixed on the false notion that if you found just the right key, you would solve your children's lives. Please see that no parent solves any grown child's life, which means you haven't failed. It's impossible to fail at what was unachievable to begin with. The mind abhors a vacuum, and you need a purposeful goal in life to fill the place where anxiety and guilt now reside.

If you seriously undertake these steps, you will go a long way toward reclaiming your own life from the self-destructive tendencies that have set in from being part of an addict's life. It's never too late to find yourself.

Is Being Gay the Issue?

Since I was six I somehow knew I was different inside. I'm twenty-one now and recognize that "it" is part of me. By "it" I mean having a queer interest in members of the same sex (I was brought up as a Christian, so you can imagine my turmoil inside). Sadly, I have been struggling to kill this part of me since I was a kid. My world was shaken when I realized that it wasn't going away.

Now I'm sure that I was genetically programmed to think and feel the way I do. I had my first bout of depression seven years ago. Currently I'm on medication to prevent its return. What direction should

I be going in? Honestly, I detest myself for being "queer."

—*Luke, 21, Singapore*

The pressing problem here isn't sexual orientation but judgment against the self. Instead of being gay, let's say you were bald. Most men are self-conscious about being bald, and it can serve as a focus for loss of self-esteem and a sense of not being masculine enough. They resent the condition and feel cheated compared to others. I hope you see that it isn't baldness that's causing such self-judgment, which can become quite obsessive and overpowering.

Being gay is more difficult to come to terms with than baldness, of course, because of society's attitudes. You don't actively detest yourself—you have passively absorbed other people's negative attitudes. Religion is part of society, and when it enters the situation, one winds up with yet another layer of disapproval, perhaps the most severe of all, since to be gay, according to Christian fundamentalists, is to put your soul in jeopardy. In your position, I would list the problems you feel inside, putting them in order of severity and then writing down a specific remedy for each. For example:

1. Feeling lonely and different

Remedy: Meet other gay people who have good self-esteem, join a gay social club, make one good gay friend, and make one good straight friend who is fine with homosexuality.

2. Self-judgment and insecurity

Remedy: Find one thing you are good at, join with people who value your accomplishments, find a confidant to share your feelings with, and make friends with somebody who can serve as a model or mentor.

3. Religious guilt

Remedy: Read a book on modern faith and gay tolerance, find a gay friend who is also Christian, and seek out a gay pastor.

4. Sexual dissatisfaction

Remedy: Join a gay group that is about something besides sex (hiking, movies, dancing, hobbies), read about heroes and pioneers of gay liberation, identify with strong role models who have successfully combined sex and love.

There are many more issues I could have included, but the point is first to get you out of yourself so that you can form less self-destructive beliefs about being gay, and, second, to use those outside contacts to build up your sense of self. You are a unique person with unique value in this world. It doesn't matter whether genes, upbringing, predisposition, or early behavior contributed to your having a gay identity. This is your main life challenge, here and now. A lot depends on confronting the challenge head-on with a positive outcome in mind. I have faith that you can.

A Depressed Spouse

My husband becomes depressed every year, and the episode typically lasts two months. The trigger that makes the depression pop up is usually a family gathering or a party with friends. He always compares himself unfavorably with everybody else. (In general he has low self-esteem.) I love my husband dearly, but he also starts drinking when he is depressed. Even though friends advise me to walk out, I can't bear the thought of him struggling alone. The hardest part is that when he feels good again, he refuses to go to therapy, read books, or meditate. But I know that there is always a next depression, and a next, and a next. What should I do?

—*Lisa, 38, Amsterdam*

Your situation is very common among those who must live with cyclical depression. We tend to think of bipolar depression swinging rapidly between black despair and manic elation. But there are other kinds of cycles, such as the one your husband is experiencing—and taking you with him.

In cyclical depression it is also common for sufferers to say, "I'm fine, there's nothing wrong," when they enter the up part of the cycle. They want to hear nothing about treatment or prevention. When they sink into the down part of the cycle, many tend to self-medicate with alcohol. I'm not mentioning this to make you feel that your difficulties are any the less for fitting a pattern. A regular MD and perhaps even a psychiatrist may not be enough. They tend to regard this condition as so hard to treat therapeutically that the only remedy they offer is antidepressants (which, sadly, the patient almost always throws away as soon as he feels good again).

Let's turn to the only aspect of this situation that you have any control over, which is your own participation. Let go of any illusion that you are "helping" the depressed person in your life. You are maintaining the status quo. Therefore it is up to you to ask the essential questions:

1. Is this something I can fix?
2. Is this something I must put up with?
3. Is this something I have to walk away from?

Because of your love and loyalty to your husband, I sense that you rely on number 2, and that reliance has made you codependent with his depression. I am not saying you are his enabler. Rather, you have adapted to his needs, and adaptation can only go so far. That is why you dread the next occurrence and feel more drained by each one. It's time for him to adapt to your needs, too. Instead of pleading for him to get help when he doesn't want to, start asserting what you actually want and need. Leave depression out of it as much as you can. What if he had a debilitating chronic illness instead? It would be reasonable to say one of the following things:

- I can't handle it all by myself.
- My well-being is also important.
- I am deeply sympathetic, but I can't be your constant lifeline. You must look out for yourself, too.
- I want to relate to the part of you that isn't sick. Please help me.
- I can't take all this denial. We have a problem in common.
- Once we talk through the problem and begin to be honest about it, as a couple we need to work together toward a solution. In that solution, both of us must find relief.

I hope you will begin to see that you have adapted too far for your own good. I don't join your friends in saying that you should walk out (although I hope you can find time for yourself apart from this problem; your friends are right that you deserve a life). I want you to reclaim your life with your husband, not without him. There has to be a balance, and right now the balance seems to be favoring him and his way of life too much.

A Dharma Bum?

My problem is an eighteen-year-old son who doesn't think that he needs to work or go to school. He says he just wants "to be" and that "the less you do, the more you get done." How can my husband and I inspire our son to realize that he must do something in order to survive while at the same time not going against his spiritual ideals?

—*Kathy, 39, Des Moines, Iowa*

I'm afraid that your dilemma is going to bring a lot of rueful smiles to readers. What you're asking about is a spoiled child who has his parents wrapped around his little finger. At eighteen, young people are trying on new identities and throwing them off again. Only time and maturity will tell us what kind of adult your son will turn into, and what he will do with his life.

You are at a delicate crux, also, because you can't keep coddling him like a child, yet you can't place adult expectations on your son, either. Try moving in that direction, however. I know it's difficult. In this family the idealistic ones are the parents. The child is doing everything he can to remain as dependent as possible. At the very least, you need to inform him about the facts of life: go to school or support yourself. The alternative is to keep treading water with nobody being the happier for it.

Overpopulation of Souls

I've always wondered how souls multiply. If, in fact, we are reincarnated, where do new souls come from and how did there get to be six billion of them on this planet?

—*Sally, 32, Silver Spring, Maryland*

You'd be surprised how often this question comes up, usually in the spirit of "gotcha." Skeptics say, "There are twice as many people in the world as fifty years ago. If all have a soul, and souls are immortal, there can't be more souls than previously. Therefore, reincarnation must be wrong." I notice that you are asking in a friendlier spirit, so here are my candid thoughts.

First, reincarnation isn't being tested by this question. For all we know, souls may be released in some kind of order that human beings cannot fathom. Maybe there's an endless supply in an infinite Pez dispenser. The rhythm of soul birth isn't our concern. All we know is that each of us is here, doing the best we can to evolve.

Second, the ego is used to thinking in terms of "I," or the separate self. But let's set aside the ego for a moment. Your soul is your deepest consciousness, the source of your awareness. To me, consciousness is a singular that has no plural. One piece of gold can be made into many gold ornaments, one fire makes many flames, one ocean many waves. Souls are patterns of movement and behavior in a single consciousness. Whether we call it the mind of God or the womb of creation, this single source can give rise to as many souls as the universe calls forth, just as the ocean can have a few waves or many without depleting itself. To be fully conscious is a twofold state. You see yourself as an individual, but you also belong to the unity known as mind.

Recession Blues

This was the year the roof fell in. Within a matter of months my husband and I separated. We declared bankruptcy and lost our business, a winery and distillery. Now I try to cope as a single parent living in a house that is about to be foreclosed on. I'm about to turn fifty, and there are moments when I feel completely lost. Mostly, however, I try to be optimistic and believe that my new journey will be an opportunity to find my life's true purpose. I want nothing more than to provide a secure and happy future for my children. People like me and respond to my positive energy. Surely there's an open door for me. My question is, how do I keep that door open?

—*Sara, 49, British Columbia*

I can assure you that your letter has sent a shudder through many hearts. In the current recession, older workers who thought that they were nearing the fulfillment of their careers find instead that the bottom has dropped out. They are poorly prepared for the loss of job or home or savings—all the safety nets we provide for ourselves in a working lifetime.

To open a new door, I think we must fall back on the adage about Nature abhorring a vacuum. Right now you have a space inside that contains the following: regret, disappointment, nostalgia for better times, hope for the future, anxiety over the future, self-esteem, and self-doubts. In other words, there's a disorganized tangle of conflicts. Shadow energies are coming up to make you feel afraid. The instability of your outer life is mirrored by inner instability as well.

You need to create space for clarity, inspiration, and new beginnings. You already possess the life skills for all of that. The problem is that so much is swirling around inside that no clarity is possible, or it only comes by fits and starts. Realize that you are in crisis mode. You cannot ask everything of yourself. Where are outside helpers, support, and most of all, where is your husband? I know he has his own anxieties, but he was part of the collapse that led to this crisis. He should be part of the path that leads out of it. Asking you to bear the burden alone is inexcusable.

I'm afraid that you also need to be tough-minded right now. Go to those you helped in the past and make it known, in no uncertain terms, that you need support during this crisis. Don't be brave; don't be a martyr; don't fall into victimization and the wishful thinking that comes packed with it. Look at yourself as if you were another person—someone you know well who needs sound, rational advice. What would you tell her? Being objective helps to clear out the confused swirl of emotions that tug one way and another day after day.

You have a good sense of your core self; that comes through clearly when you write. It's the core self that gets people through crises. Externals come second. Yes, the recession and the blows it has delivered to the lives of good, well-deserving people are real. But inner resilience and the ability to bounce back are personal qualities, and they prove decisive in cases like yours. Align yourself with someone who has this kind of resilience so that your own can be strengthened. Find another oak to weather the storm with you. Anyone who is in touch with his or her core self will always respond. Before you worry about staying positive, take steps, however small, to get out of crisis mode. Once you orient yourself realistically in that direction, the doors that need to open will begin to do so.

Can I Become Enlightened?

Is it man's purpose to seek and reach enlightenment? What are the obstacles to getting there, and how does one overcome them? I preach positive thinking to everyone around me, but sometimes I find myself feeling hopeless. I can't get out of this rut. Please help.

—*Claudine, 41, Sherman Oaks, California*

You have asked two questions, but let me see if we can link them. Positive thinking is very good, even necessary, in order to have a hopeful vision of life. Your vision is of enlightenment, and nothing could be more positive. Having found your vision, however, you don't have to force yourself to think positively all the time. That is an artificial way to approach the mind. I find that if you don't force your mind, it works more naturally and with less stress.

Now, having set your goal at enlightenment, how do you get there? First, let's not think in terms of obstacles. Enlightenment is the product of personal growth. When a rose is growing in your garden, aiming for the day it will give forth a glorious blossom, it doesn't think, "What are the obstacles to overcome before I can flower?" It simply grows, taking the good and the bad as they come, with the assurance that one day the flower will appear.

Yet roses bloom best with rich soil, lots of nourishment, and tender care. The same holds true for you. Only two things are needed on the spiritual path: a vision of the goal, and the means to expand your awareness. Whatever enlightenment may be—and many traditions describe it differently—every step toward enlightenment is a step of self-awareness. Throughout history, spiritual traditions point to meditation as the single most important tool for self-awareness. As you become more aware, however, not everything that reveals itself is positive. Life is a mixed blessing, and everyone has a shadow self.

But no matter how difficult some aspect of your life may be, it need not serve as an obstacle to spirit. Your body may face obstacles, and so may your psyche. Deal with these the best way you can find; in other words, lead a normal life with support from family, friends, and others who are spiritually minded. But spirit is about awareness, and as long as you know that, the opportunity for expanded consciousness will always appear. Sometimes it appears in meditation, sometimes as a new insight, at other times as guides and teachers who appear to help us. Let your higher self be the ultimate guide and keep firm in knowing that the whole path takes place in consciousness.

Her Unruly Son

My twenty-two-year-old son lives at home, going to college part time and working part time. He never volunteers to help out with chores, to cook a meal, or wash the dishes. He comes and goes in a surly mood, without saying hello or good-bye. Toward me he takes a superior attitude, as if he's in charge. Yet he sits around playing video games every spare moment. I'm divorced and a single mom. How can I get my son to be kinder to me? Frankly, if he just pretended, that would be good enough at this point.

—*Audrey, 46, Oak Park, Illinois*

Your son is extending his adolescence as far as he can stretch it. The attitudes you describe—including the superior air, the addiction to video games, avoidance of chores, and disregard for you—are well known to every parent of a sixteen-year-old. They are pretty inexcusable in a twenty-two-year-old, however. In addition, your situation is compounded by two aggravating factors. Your son learned his callous attitude from his father, I'm afraid. And you are experiencing the downside of being a single mom, which is that you have become too dependent on your son for emotional feedback and too ready to let him linger in immaturity.

What this comes down to is that you are no good for him and he is no good for you. This is a mutually unbeneficial relationship. As the adult, it's up to you to face reality as it applies to you. Get a life outside your son. Force yourself to let him grow up. Stop paying so much attention to him; stop burdening him with your disappointments and failed expectations. I know this is a strong dose of medicine, but it will heal you in the end.

As for your son, your worry is well placed. He isn't in a good position to grow up. He has little motivation to do so, and he's too immature to see the downfall that awaits him if he refuses to grow up. Your role is to help open his eyes. First, he needs a strong talk from a man he respects. This man needs to deliver some hard truths. Second, he needs a role model who fits the kind of person he should be growing into.

I can't tell you what kind of role model is exactly right. This will take some clear-headed thinking on your part. At twenty-two, many young adults can't identify their strengths and weaknesses. They need more experience, perhaps some mentoring. No doubt that's true of your son. But find a man whose career and life choices will make your son say, "I want to be like that. I can be like that." Without such a figure in his life—or in the life of any young adult—the prospect for the future is more aimless drifting.

Youth at a Crossroads

I am having a really hard time with choices when it comes to finding a direction in life. I want to do something I love and am passionate about, but I haven't figured out what that is yet. In the meantime I'm not willing to compromise my ideals just to be practical. School and work felt meaningless to me, so I dropped out and spent a year not going out, basically just reading books on spirituality and psychology in hopes that I could find myself.

Now I feel more grounded spiritually, but in my practical life I haven't accomplished anything. I want to trust that everything is as it should be. Even so, there are times when I feel dead inside. I have no aspirations; I don't even know why I'm here.

—*Annie, 24, New Haven, Connecticut*

Your letter gets more and more negative as it goes on, culminating in a starling statement: I feel dead inside. So what started out as one thing—a letter from an idealistic young person who has postponed her identity crisis—winds up sounding like a letter from someone who is acutely depressed. Therefore, the only way you can get an answer is to go inside and find it. You've read a lot of spiritual books. The seed is sown. Now it's time to let some seeds sprout.

To find out which ones, here are five questions to ask yourself. Write them down and keep the paper available, because you will need to ask each question every day until it is answered. I'll list the questions first and then tell you a special way to answer them, because the method is as important as the answers:

1. Am I depressed and sick of my life?
2. Am I drifting because I know something perfect is waiting just over the horizon?
3. Is today going the way I want it to?
4. When I look around, does my life tell me who I am? What do I see in the reflection of the outer world?
5. If I could jump ahead five years and meet myself, who would I meet?

These are questions that get asked during the identity crisis of one's early twenties. They are always asked in confusion, because late adolescence isn't quite over and fully fledged adulthood has not quite begun. People experience their identity crises in very different ways. They tend to bring out what we most fear and what we most dream of. This is a time for love, ideals, a career, growing confidence, and the excitement of taking flight.

That's the ideal, but of course many people experience

other elements of the identity crisis: a paralyzing sense of indecision, loss of self-confidence, panic that old behaviors that worked in your teens no longer work, and a frightening sense of emptiness. Right now you are mired in the negative side of finding your true identity. So let's eliminate the negative and let the positive part of your life start to guide you.

That's where the five questions come in. Pull out your list in the morning. Read each question, then close your eyes and wait for an answer. Don't force; don't expect anything. If you hear a lot of chatter in your mind, exhale and mentally ask this chatter to stop for a moment so you can have a clear mind. Whatever answer you receive after a few minutes, that's today's answer. Move on to the next question. Once you have your five answers, go on and enjoy your day. Don't think about the questions again. Don't return to them. You have done your job for the day. The rest is for enjoyment.

Repeat this procedure every day. One day—no one can predict when—one of the answers will seem totally right to you. This means that your true self has delivered the answer. Don't jump for joy just yet. Come back two more times and see if the same answer returns. If so, cross that question off your list. Proceed for as long as it takes until you have five good and true answers. What have you done? You've caught up with where you need to be. Because you are young, your answers may change next year, but what you want is answers for right now. They will serve to get you out of your rut.

A Hopeless Search

I am constantly in search of "something" and have wound up exhausted, lost, and sad. I thought surviving cancer would keep me on track and living simply. It did for a while, but now I am back searching and hoping again. I pray and talk to God, angels, and guides, but I think I am making it all up or just fantasizing. Where do I go from here? I know there is more, but what? Where?

—*Janet, 60, Sacramento, California*

Perhaps we should begin with your age. At sixty it's only natural to want validation in your life. You should be able to look inside and find a set of core values by which to live. Whatever that something is that wants to unfold, it does so on the basis of the core self that you have established.

In your case core seems weak or absent, which means one of two things: either you have postponed the work of establishing a stable, meaningful self or that self was weakened by trauma, hurt, and disappointment. I can't tell you which is true—perhaps there's an element of both. In any event, the way forward is the same. The "more" that you are seeking is you. It isn't a revelation delivered by angels or an epiphany from God.

I don't mean to imply that you shouldn't seek a connection with the sacred. But if you spent years trying to chop down a tree with a butter knife, wouldn't you realize that you haven't gone about it the right way? In your case, the reason that inspiration from many sources hasn't stuck is that you haven't been realistic about what it means to be on the spiritual path. Beyond anything else, it's the path to reality. So you must become realistic about your life and begin to do the work of finding yourself. The reality you seek is as close as breathing. There's no need to search for it in the sky or the wind.

The Outsider

I was born with physical defects, and over my life I've had thirty-six surgeries. When I was small, I didn't really know there was anything wrong with me. Once I went to elementary school, however, things became very difficult. The things the other kids said were awful—"Scarface, Frankenstein, you'll only have a boyfriend if he puts a sack over your head." My mom was oblivious to my issues. My stepfather sat me on his lap and said, "You'll never be beautiful, so be smart instead." The trouble is, even though I did well in school, he still called me stupid.

I know that I am smart, caring, and a really kind and loving person. But when I walk into a room, I see people staring and doing double takes. Telling them why I look this way only confirms how ashamed

I already feel about myself—it's a catch-22. How do I win? I have been in therapy, and still I cannot let this go.

—*Leonie, 39, Baltimore, Maryland*

Your issues, painful as they are, can be treated. If your therapist hasn't made headway, you need to talk to someone who can. The essential problem is that you are carrying into adulthood strong beliefs imprinted by your parents. Your mother was unable to overcome her guilt at having an imperfect child, and your stepfather fortified her feelings instead of helping to resolve them. Before you had a self, when you were so little that you had no choice but to attach your identity to your mother, you were conditioned in totally the wrong way.

I congratulate you for winning your life back. Through adversity you became a better person than all your tormentors from the past, including those who raised you. On the basis of your own strength, your healing depends on reaching the following realizations:

- It wasn't your job to make your mother happy.
- It wasn't your fault that she couldn't forgive herself.
- You didn't fail as a child, because there was no way you could have won. Your parents simply were who they were.
- You need a new set of parents, and they exist within you. These parents consist of your own sense of worthiness.

- There is a way to let go of past pain.
- It's safe to be different. You don't have to keep defending your right to exist.

Unless you find a therapist who explicitly works on these core issues, there's no point in going back. At the same time, please write down these points and begin to work on yourself. Healing is always within reach. You have gone a long way. Now you've reached the nitty-gritty. It may be harder to heal, yet the task has been accomplished many times, and once you find the right guidance, you will accomplish it, too.

My Bad Boss

Eight months ago I resigned from my job because my boss was a bully and disrespectful of me. When I brought this up to her superiors, they did nothing to correct the situation. Now she has given me a bad reference to prospective new employers. I can't seem to get away from her. How do I move on?
—*Celine, 58, Minneapolis, Minnesota*

There's a short-term answer to your dilemma, and a long-term answer as well. The short-term answer is to explain the friction to prospective employers quite openly in your job interview. Be forthcoming and adult, without blaming your old boss or making excuses—employers will pick up on your honesty. Offer to give other references from your old job if you want, but I think no one will miss who you are just because of a nasty reference.

The long-term answer requires some inner work on yourself. I sense that you feel wronged and hurt, but also offended and perhaps guilty, as if you had provoked her bad behavior or failed to make it get better. These feelings are the strings tying you to this old boss. You need to talk about them with a mature person who will understand and compassionately guide you. No good will come if you stew in your own juices and keep reliving the past, trying to make yourself feel better. You have real wounds inside, even if they are invisible. Take steps to find a way to heal them. I hope this helps.

Longing to Have Another Baby

My husband and I have a beautiful girl who just turned four. I want another child, but my husband doesn't. We have been fighting a lot, and now he is having trouble performing in the bedroom. To me, this is just another way to avoid what I want so badly. I can't believe he is not feeling what I am.
—*Marianne, 36, Denver, Colorado*

You need to take the pressure off your husband and yourself. The stress is making him limp. May I suggest a modified time-out? Sit down and write a letter to him listing all your reasons for wanting a new baby and expressing yourself as fully as you can. Ask him to write you a letter expressing his reasons for not wanting another child, expressing all his doubts.

After you each read the other's letter, in private, put them away for four months. Don't bring up the subject again. Let time do its work. At the end of four months, take out the letters again. Read only yours, and ask yourself if your position has changed. Your husband should do the same. If neither of you has changed, put the letters away again for four months. But if, as I suspect, there is a softening of either position, talk it over. If there is still no agreement, write new letters. I think this will work if you really promise to leave the subject alone in the interim.

Family Feud

My grown-up son and my husband had a heated argument over Christmas, and even though my husband has apologized and asked for a second chance, my son and his fiancée refuse to have anything to do with either of us. My son blames us for everything bad in his life. We are devastated, but he is controlling the situation. We had a good family until this happened.

—*Carlene, 56, New Hampshire*

Can a good family be torn apart by a single argument, however bitter? There is hidden resentment here, and it's been hiding for a while. Your son's feelings are totally justified as he views them, and totally unjustified as you and your husband view them. You have arrived at an impasse. When that happens, the best thing to do is back away. Having a third party, his fiancée, in between only hardens the distance between you.

Since you are fifty-six, I assume your son is a full-fledged adult. He may not be acting like one. The chances are that he is being emotionally immature—his petulance sounds adolescent as you describe it. Yet, as you say, he controls the situation. He is faced with that age-old question, "Can you ever go home again?"

The answer is yes, but there's a catch. You can go home again after you have made peace with your past. I wish I had better news for you, but your son isn't at peace. He isn't reaching out to you for advice or healing. I wish he would. But for now, let him have his distance. Put no pressure on him of any sort. Be polite and kind on the phone if he calls. Eventually he will remember the good things about you and his father. When that happens, it will be up to him to make the first gesture of reconciliation.

Enlightened or Happy?

Are enlightenment and happiness the same thing?
—*Dee, 52, Boston*

The simplicity and directness of your question are refreshing. But I'm being put on the spot a bit by not knowing why you ask this question. If you feel that enlightenment is a good way to be happy, such hopes are probably an illusion. Enlightenment means the awakening to full consciousness, a state where the concerns of the ego no longer exist. That is a faraway state by any measure.

But to get to enlightenment, a person must walk the spiritual path, and indeed such a journey does increase one's happiness. That's because of where the path leads, which is closer and closer to your true self. The true self lies at the core of the self you call "me." But it isn't overshadowed by the everyday ups and downs of life. Your true self has no agenda. It is content simply to *be*. In being, there is a quality of bliss that is innocent and simple. We all experience it in moments when we are in a state of peaceful enjoyment—it's like gazing at the blue sky on a spring day without the slightest troubling thought inside.

Not every sky will be blue and not every day is springtime. So on the spiritual path a person learns to find this kind of happiness without needing nice things to happen on the outside. Rather, you find happiness by being who you really are. This isn't mystical. Young children are happy being who they are. The trick is to regain such a state when you are grown and have seen the light and dark sides of life. I encourage you to try the path for yourself. For guidance, I've written a recent book, *The Ultimate Happiness Prescription*, which talks about the path to happiness in detail.

When Is It Cheating?

I have been married or living with the same man for six years and together we are raising three teenage children. My husband cheated on me prior to our wedding with the mother of his youngest child. Because this woman is the mother of his child, she is still a part of our lives. I recently found out that my husband has been calling her in secret. His excuse is that he isn't cheating and that I need to get over it. But I feel betrayed. Should I leave him? Do I have a right to feel this way? I'm confused.

—*Sherry, 35, Los Angeles*

Almost anyone would share your response. Cheating is more than an action, it's an attitude. To stop cheating requires the man (let's assume we are talking about cheating husbands for the moment) to change his attitudes first. Only then does changing his behavior really mean anything. If only the behavior changes, the result will be superficial. His wife will always be nervous and insecure about a relapse, as you are right now.

I don't insist that "once a cheater, always a cheater," but that saying was born out of bitter experience. Here are the ingredients that go into a cheater's psyche:

- The more women I have, the sexier I feel.
- Men aren't designed to be monogamous.

- Sleeping with other women gives me breathing room in my marriage. It's like a vacation.
- The other women don't mean anything. I don't see why my wife is so upset.
- A real man can satisfy more than one woman.
- I do whatever I can get away with.
- I have a right to be myself, and this is who I am.
- It's easier to run to another woman than to face problems with my wife.
- It's my wife's fault, really. She doesn't satisfy me.
- I am open-minded, and I can't help it if other people, including my wife, aren't.

I am not saying that your husband harbors all these attitudes—no cheater does—but your letter indicates quite a few. He has made them part of himself. It's his story, and he's sticking to it. Can you make him change his story out of love for you? No. If he loved you enough to change his story, he wouldn't cheat in the first place.

I don't want to sound gloomy. Have hope, but follow up on your hope. If your husband is telling the truth and no longer cheating, you need to take responsibility and deal with your own insecurity. It's inevitable that having a cheating spouse is devastating to one's own sense of being desirable, worthy, protected, nurtured, and cherished. You must use your vulnerable state to acquire those things in yourself. But if you undertake such a journey to heal, the first step is that your husband must agree to change his attitude. Otherwise you are trying to empty the bathtub while he keeps dumping in more water.

Lingering Grief

My only son died ten years ago in a roll-over high-way accident. He was twenty-three and my shining star. We both worked in the ER of our local hospital. His father and I have been divorced since my son was three. After this crushing loss I am just beginning to breathe again. I have post-traumatic stress disorder from this, and my spirituality was deeply shaken. I feel very disconnected from everything and everyone, although most people don't sense it. I live in a very good place on the Yellowstone River and I find comfort watching the wildlife on the river, especially in the winter when the eagles are here. But my mental suffering hasn't ended, and I don't know what to do.

—*Brenda, 63, Montana*

Grief is a devastating condition under circumstances like yours, and you have my heartfelt sympathy. But I am also going to be realistic, which requires some bluntness. You were living through your son, as so often happens with single mothers. He became part of you, and when he died, part of your identity went with him. This happens in close relationships where two people create a single person, each filling the gaps and holes in the other's psyche.

In time, a twenty-three-year-old son would have found a way to separate himself, and although the process would have been difficult, you would retain his love. With the sudden separation due to accidental death you were wrenched apart, and the numbness, confusion, alienation, depression, and "walking dead" feelings that you now have are the result of not being able to assemble a whole person out of the fragments left behind.

For you, reading spiritual books, although comforting, hasn't led in the right direction; they have made you more indwelling and isolated. I'm glad that you have the balm of Nature to comfort you, but a big practical project lies ahead of you: putting a self back together without the missing pieces from your son. Here are the major steps in such a project:

1. Decide that you want to be a complete person.

2. Recognize that your son cannot replace the gaps he once filled.

3. Judge yourself as worthy to be happy and deserving of a rich future.

4. Connect with people who want you to be whole and fulfilled.

5. Ask the most mature and fulfilled people in your life to help and support you.

6. Find a mentor or therapist who can mirror your progress and setbacks realistically.

7. Come to terms with the residues of memory, loss, grief, and woundedness.

8. Walk away from the role of victim once and for all.

9. Learn to honor your grief while giving a greater place to love.

Write down these nine steps and seriously consider them. Passively waiting for time to heal you won't work. You must work to become objective and realistic. You must be fully committed to reclaiming your own life. If you can do that, you will be a living memorial to your son instead of a living gravestone. A living memorial is one that he would be proud of.

Feeling Blue—or Is It More?

I have been trying to change my thought process to reflect more positivity. Negative thoughts do come, but I want to push them aside and not pay them any mind. I am doing okay most of the time, but there are moments of depression. I am not on medication and don't want to be. What is a good first step to change this situation and begin to create my own reality, because I know that I can?

Jennifer, 47, Northern Virginia

Whenever someone says "I'm depressed," usually a reason follows, but your letter is quite guarded. You only reveal that you struggle with negative thoughts and want reassurance that you can be positive again—this implies a state of insecurity, self-doubt, and feeling unsafe. Why do you fear that you won't be okay?

The answer to that lies within yourself, so the first step is to look at yourself closely in the mirror and find a reason for your depressed state, whenever it occurs, that you can trust. For example,

- I'm stuck in a bad situation.
- Someone else is controlling me.
- I feel powerless to change my circumstances.
- I feel like a victim.
- I feel that I will never succeed.
- I am in drastic lack.
- I have had mood difficulties for a long time, but can't seem to figure out why.

These aren't ready-made answers. I don't want you to suddenly apply them to yourself. But if any do apply, they indicate a way out. For example, bad circumstances and situations that make you feel trapped can be changed. If you have to, you should walk away until you land somewhere safer. Likewise, if someone else is controlling your life, you need to reclaim it for yourself. If you feel like a failure or hopeless, you need to address issues of self-esteem. If your moods turn negative for no reason you can find, a doctor's care is indicated.

The tendency with depression, because it makes you feel helpless and hopeless, is to cloud the truth. The truth that you need to glimpse is that a way out exists. I am not so sure you are depressed. My sense is that you feel insecure and controlled for reasons you haven't disclosed. Perhaps you don't feel safe enough even to divulge the problem in a letter?

The Doormat

I have a longtime friend who is always in the midst of a crisis. She calls me to complain about her loneliness, and she can't think of one thing to be grateful for. She is on medication for bipolar disorder and also drinks heavily. She also smokes, involves herself with married men, and is about to lose her home after spending a large inheritance. I have listened with a sympathetic ear for years now, and I care about her well-being, but recently I have begun to feel like an enabler. Her calls are emotionally draining, but my suggestions about being more positive cause resentment. What should I do?

—*Selma, 35, Chicago*

Readers must be shaking their heads, wondering why you want to be a doormat for someone else to walk over. You have wasted years indulging your friend's many self-inflicted problems, a role that's as thankless as any I can think of. You've permitted yourself to count for very little while she magnetizes every conversation to herself. Now, to top it off, you're looking for ways to feel guilty about not doing enough.

Please, try to develop the inner quality known as strength. Otherwise, even if you walk away, you will be somebody's doormat again. The first place to start is with boundaries. Your friend trampled on you because you let her, and when you—feebly and gently—stood up for yourself, she was outraged. Let her go her own way. Learn when to say no by first checking on how you feel. If someone is taking advantage, the feeling is never good. Notice when it doesn't feel good, and put up limits, such as "I can only talk for a few minutes." Then, when you find that your limits are respected, you will discover that, good as it feels to help others, it feels just as good to be strong.

Should She Go or Stay?

I married my husband seventeen years ago, even though I wasn't in love with him. As a single mother, I wanted my young children to have a real family; I told myself that it was "the right thing to do." Now that my daughter is old enough to leave home and my son is fast on her heels, I feel as though my world is closing in on me. All I have left is a lukewarm marriage—not so bad that I have to leave, but not so good that I can enjoy having done well with my life. I feel as though I settled, and settled miserably. Help me to know if this is just a menopausal phase or an outcry from my soul.

—May, 46, Seattle

When people bring up various problems, one category stands out. Whatever the issue, whatever the conflict, at some level the person already knows what to do. They are basically asking for permission to do it. You fall into that category. Nobody asks loaded questions like "Should I go back to being bored and miserable?" unless they already know the answer. In your view, what would make a marriage bad enough to leave it—having your husband set you on fire?

There's a touching aspect to your situation, which is that you value duty—doing the right thing—over happiness. That's very old-fashioned and in its way noble. But you've wound up with a devil's bargain in this marriage, and one has to wonder why your husband wanted a wife who didn't love him. I think it's obvious that the two of you don't communicate on any level of intimacy or emotional honesty. So getting out of the marriage may be the most honest thing you've done in many years. I applaud you for waking up and smelling the coffee.

The Problem with Life Is . . .

I'm bothered by the expression "may all beings be blessed." How can all beings be blessed at the same time? The life of one being will sometimes involve the death of another. If you look around, life feeds on life in order to survive. Even vegetarians who wear no leather must claim some part of the earth as their space and banish or kill the insects that might have lived there. Does one need to make a distinction between physical blessing and spiritual blessing to justify this seeming paradox?

—*Lee Ann, 54, El Paso, Texas*

My first instinct is to ask if you are a worrywart. You don't have to frustrate yourself by asking ultimate questions for which there are no answers. A blessing expresses warm feelings, wishes, and benediction. Blessings weren't made up by philosophers with PhDs. But on reflection I realize that your question is more indirect. You aren't worried about vegetarians hurting the carrots they pull out of the ground. You are worried about the existence of cruelty and pain, the kind of pain that every life brings with it.

The issue of suffering isn't resolved for you, and I admire that. But let's focus on *your* suffering rather than whatever afflicts life itself. If you experience your own life as something full of risk, danger, unfairness, inhumanity, and so on, that means you are a feeling person. Having me resolve a point of morality isn't going to erase those feelings. What will? Taking your empathy seriously and doing one of two things. Either go out and help others who are in suffering and pain or begin to walk the path of self-awareness. These aren't incompatible choices, of course.

I think you will find, once you begin to help others, that suffering doesn't kill the human spirit. We are here to question and yearn. If we deal with our nature in a healthy way, this yearning makes us grow. If we don't deal with our nature in a healthy way, we sit around and worry with no results but more worry.

Putting Up with a Grouch

As my husband is growing older, he is becoming a grouch, to the point that I don't want to go out in public with him. He finds fault with every little thing, and he can't resist haranguing me and anyone else within earshot. At restaurants he bawls out the server. He uses terrible language over the phone. As for me, he criticizes the smallest incident. Two years ago I wrote him a letter saying that I wouldn't tolerate his bad behavior any longer. If he didn't change, our relationship would come to an end. After that, things went well until six months ago, when the quick temper and rude behavior returned. Believe it or not, I still love my husband, but I don't like him. What should I do?

—*Elizabeth, 65, Detroit*

I hear a voice inside me, and inside most readers, muttering, "Walk out on the SOB." Your husband is set in his ways, even with temporary improvements. But you cannot leave until you make some basic decisions. The first is the most important: Is this a situation you can fix? To answer yes, the following must be true:

- Your husband recognizes and acknowledges the problem.
- He regrets losing his temper.
- He asks for help.

- He wants to include you in the healing process.
- You see signs of improvement when you take action.

In your case, the last point is cause for hope. You saw signs of improvement when you presented your husband with an ultimatum. He took you seriously, but now he's had a relapse. Can you get through to him again? Ultimatums stop working after the first time; they turn into empty threats once you prove that you won't leave.

Also, I sense that you are a people-pleaser. It may take professional guidance to steer your decision. Only after a counselor or therapist helps you to see that fixing it is hopeless will you find the strength to extricate yourself without guilt and remorse. I can assure you that this man's life is going to go downhill fast without you.

I'd also like to mention a bit more about his anger. At his age, I assume he's retired. Men who leave a job that meant everything to them wind up, through no fault of their own, feeling bitter and wronged. It's this internal bitterness that causes the outbursts. He feels "better" by making others feel worse. His sense of loss is compensated for by showing others that he is in distress. But since he doesn't want to admit that he is in distress, he displays his hidden feelings as anger. If you feel that a sudden personality change has occurred, consider having medical tests run also.

There are other ingredients that come to mind, such as his need to be right. This is a symptom of control issues. Perhaps at his work he had authority and could tell others how to do their job. Perhaps he was always a finicky perfectionist or someone who never could be pleased. Age may have exacerbated those tendencies. This happens because older people often let down their social boundaries. Their excuse for turning boorish is "I'm too old to care what other people think." That's sad but quite common.

I hope I've given you enough information to make the right choices, none of them easy. You don't need to live with an insufferable grouch who won't admit that he's the one who needs to get right, not the waiter who spills coffee. Don't lapse back into inertia. If you examine yourself closely, that's how you will find the means to make some hard choices.

Love Jitters

I've been in a happy relationship for sixteen months and have never been this much in love, ever. He loves me unconditionally and tells me so every chance he gets. So why do I feel so insecure? Why, all of a sudden, do I panic that I'm going to lose him to someone else? I don't want to mess this up over negative feelings that I cannot get over.

—*Laura, 43, New Jersey*

Well, that's how love is. It creates pain and joy at the same time, and for the same reason, because deeper aspects of ourselves are brought to light. The openness that love brings, if you are lucky, isn't just being open to the best things in life. You also feel like a child again, and that brings a sense of need that is very vulnerable.

I also paused over your words "unconditional love." Nobody loves you unconditionally who has only known you for sixteen months. It's a lovely promise and a desirable goal, but you're not there yet. Some part of you knows this. You aren't a teenager, and you've fallen in and out of love before. So my advice is to look at your feelings as the normal turmoil of love and press ahead. When someone asks, "How do I find the right one?" my answer is "Don't look for the right one. Be the right one." The same holds true for you.

Look at It This Way

When I look around, I see that there's too much pain and suffering caused by evildoing, catastrophe, and economic crisis. Is danger hovering around us all the time, or is there another way to look at things?
—*Len, 31, Portland, Oregon*

I'm sure you realize that there is another way to look at things, so the real question is how to adopt another way. You can't talk yourself into seeing sunshine on a rainy day. If you try, you are deluding yourself. Many people, thinking of themselves as realists, feel the same about good and evil. They don't want to take their eyes off the negative aspects of life, because realism demands that we take the bitter with the sweet.

Yet who is to say that the bitter is more real than the sweet? If your vision of life contains love and peace, if you yourself have renounced violence, if you set yourself on the spiritual path, these things don't mean you aren't a realist. They mean you aim for a higher reality. I don't mean God, although I am not excluding religion. We are talking about hidden potential. Human nature is divided; it contains both darkness and light. You can choose to accept the darkness and lament it, or you can choose to expand the light until the darkness no longer dominates.

There is no getting around this choice, which is highly personal. I know that millions of people are alienated and disenchanted. They sit passively watching the latest reports of violence and catastrophes, corruption and misdeeds, float by on the evening news. But the old adage is true: one candle is enough to cause the darkness to go away. Once you choose to raise your own awareness, you will have done the most you can to defeat the dark side of human nature and to discover that a higher reality can actually be found and lived.

Pattern of Abuse

I have been divorced for almost five years. I was married for twenty, but my ex was emotionally abusive. The first relationship I got into after my divorce ended badly because of [my lover's] alcoholism. Now I'm afraid that I will wind up in a disastrous

relationship again. How can I break the pattern
and move on?
—*Rhonda, 46, Grand Rapids, Michigan*

Getting sucked into abusive relationships involves
two tendencies that are intimately connected. The first is
the tendency to overlook warning signs. People aren't closed
books or secret codes. They give off signals. They behave
in indicative ways. If you don't ignore the warning signs,
it's not that hard to see who is going to be abusive, controlling, self-centered, uncaring, dominating, cruel, or severely
addicted. I am not saying that the men you meet are going
to present themselves with total candor and honesty. Of
course they aren't; no one does. We show the best sides of
ourselves in social situations, particularly when we want
to win someone over.

The second tendency is to miss the signals that tell you
who is a good match for you. Missing the red flags seems
easy enough. You want to see the best in others. You think,
quite rightly, that suspicion and distrust aren't good things
to bring to a new relationship. But overlooking the good in
others is just as destructive. Because most people carry
around an image in their heads of "the right one," they dis-
miss others based on that image. Think of the men you
have rejected as boring, not good-looking enough, not rich
or smart enough, and so on when in fact their only fault
was not living up to an artificial image. This is compounded
by society's addiction to external qualities being the most
important. Dozens of beautiful, successful, charming sin-
gles have appeared on television shows that are supposed to

find perfect mates for a bachelor and bachelorette. How many happy marriages have resulted? One or two at most, and even those have yet to stand the test of time.

The critical issue, then, is how to overcome both tendencies. You want to spot the warning signs in advance, but also the hidden virtues. The ability to do these things comes naturally, but we block it in various ways. You've mentioned a big blockage, fear based on past failures and hurt. As Mark Twain once noted, a cat that has sat on a hot stove won't sit on any stove afterward, whether it is hot or not. Which is to say, you can't trust your old wounds. You must learn to be open and new as opportunities arise. You must learn to look past your ingrained image that keeps you from seeing other people as they actually are, which is always a mixture of good and bad.

Much of this comes down to ambivalence. When you can see the good and bad in someone else, how do you react? If you are mature, you accept what is good and tolerate what is bad, but only to a point. Being ambivalent isn't the same as perfect romance. It's a state of tolerance. Having reached that state, something new emerges. No longer blinded by a fantasy of perfect love, you find that you are less critical; you don't judge others as much; you have less fear and distrust. At that point you will be able to do the most important thing: you will know what you need and how to get it. Most people are confused about what they actually need, and therefore they seek it in the wrong places.

I would suggest that you need safety, security, reassurance, love, and nurturing, in that order. We can't discount the wounding relationships in your past. At a more advanced stage, when you feel safe and secure, you might look for love, compassion, and wisdom as first priorities. Having identified your needs, look at a prospective mate realistically, as someone who might fulfill your needs. Go on dates, relate for a while, and test the other person's capacities. I know how easy it is to feel that you can't place demands. You focus your energies on pleasing another. You self-consciously worry over being young enough, pretty enough, and good enough. But that is how bad relationships explode in your face. Having focused on your own shortcomings, you failed to test whether the other person actually met your needs.

Once you turn around your attention, you can begin to be realistic about who this other person is and what he has to give. I think that's the most important step, and I hope I have given you enough clues about what to look for in the future so that it isn't simply a repetition of the past.

Spiritual Grasshopper

No matter how much I work at something, no matter how much I reach for others, no matter how much I meditate, contribute, or alter my mental state, everything in my life remains the same. Nothing ever changes. I work on myself inside and outside, but my situation doesn't budge. What's wrong, and why am I stuck?

—*Danny, 50, Athens, Greece*

You are suffering from a bad case of superficiality. If I asked you to cook dinner, would you run into the kitchen, open the cupboards, and start throwing food around the room? That's what you are doing with your life. You are like a panicky bird running from one thing to the next. The tone of your letter is melodrama verging on the edge of hysteria. I suspect that you are a frazzled but charming person who dithers and frets, but gets along well enough. So my advice is to stand in front of the mirror and decide when you want to get serious. At that moment, help will come, and so will change.

What you are experiencing now is almost constant change, but it's frittering away your time. Happily, if there is a higher power, it takes care of spiritual grasshoppers, too.

What Do My Dreams Mean?

Sometimes I have dreams that mean nothing, but I often have dreams that are messages. These dreams seem to be linked to things that happen in the near future. When I dream about my oldest son, most of the time it's a warning for him, and he has been saved a few times. In December I had a dream about four people dying on the same day. Later that week it was in the news that four construction workers had died falling from a building. I wouldn't say that I have powers, but deep down I feel that something real is going on. Is it all in my head, or is there a special name for this?

—*Carla, 35, Tampa, Florida*

I agree that something is going on, but it's not always easy to find a name for it. It's even harder to make others believe in an experience they haven't had themselves. Dreams have a long history of delivering messages. At the very least they have been considered meaningful and mysterious. At present, however, the pendulum has swung the other way, and neuroscientists tend to say that dreams represent random or garbled brain activity.

If your dreams have meaning for you, isn't that enough validation? I have meaningful dreams myself. Sometimes they serve as a spur to creativity. Sometimes they comment on my current emotional state or on things that seem uncertain in the future. By their nature, dreams are personal and unpredictable.

Your dreams contain the element of premonition. You see or sense future events, usually negative events. Why? Because despite any worries about being called delusional or flaky, you have opened a channel to a subtler part of your mind. You gave yourself permission to step into the domain of intuition and insight—or perhaps we should say far sight. Be happy about this. Millions of people less open than you have sealed off the subtler levels of the mind and have no access to intuition and insight. As for the practical use of your dreams, a lot depends on what you think is acceptable. Maybe you can help more people than just your son. Or maybe this will remain a private experience. Don't resist any possibility. Let the guidance of your heart carry you to the next step.

One Level at a Time

For many years now I have been on a healing journey that becomes increasingly spiritual, and this has made me more attuned to the things that make me feel whole and right. But there is one person in my life, my common-law husband, who keeps pulling me back into the shadows of doubt and negativity. I am so confused over how I should perceive our relationship. We are raising two daughters. I don't feel an intimate connection with this man, yet I continue to stay because I feel a moral responsibility to do so. We have two young daughters to consider. I try to believe that I can achieve my own inner peace regardless of him. He thinks we represent a normal family (from the outside). He is also very concerned about his self-image, which would take a blow if we separated. Should I continue on my own personal journey while staying in an unsatisfying relationship?

—*Gloria, 31, Ontario*

Your dilemma has two levels that you have mingled, and that is the main source of your present confusion. Let's separate the two and see if some clarity can be reached.

On the first level, you live with a man to whom you are not intimately connected and who doesn't want things to change. This is a self-esteem issue. Do you feel lovable and worthy? If so, you wouldn't live with him on a false basis, pretending to be normal when every fiber in your being tells you that the reality of your relationship is dysfunctional. However, this doesn't mean that you should walk out tomorrow. Your priority should be to look at yourself and find out why you feel unlovable, unworthy, ashamed, victimized, or deserving no better than this kind of mistreatment.

I'm not suggesting that all these terms apply, but only that you need to get to the bottom of your own motives. We know his motives. He wants to keep you under his thumb. You rationalize your entrapment by using morality and citing your young daughters. In what way is it moral to raise children in an unhappy atmosphere? I think if you look a bit deeper you will see that what keeps you there is insecurity and fear. These are serious personal issues, but they can be faced, and in your case I think you must face them.

On the second level, you also want to grow spiritually. Isn't your whole life sending you a spiritual message right now? The message is "You aren't in the right place emotionally. You are settling for too little. Your awareness is dominated by resistance." Your partner is an adult, albeit a selfish and limited adult. Accept his word—he has no interest in joining you on your journey of personal growth. Maybe he feels threatened by it; maybe he thinks it's ridiculous; maybe he's just bored. But surely you can see that he's not going to support you.

Having cleared out that fantasy, you will find that beneath your wishful thinking lies a good deal of sorrow and regret. I'm very sorry for that, but to be frank, the spiritual path is all about confronting resistance and finding strength from within. Otherwise the whole enterprise easily turns into a frolic in dreamland. I'm glad that you feel sustained, at least somewhat, by your spirit, given your difficult circumstances. But your spirit doesn't want you to be trapped like this. It doesn't want you to retreat inside to some kind of mythical peace while all around you is rejection and obstacles. The positive side of the reflections you are being given is that your life can be much better.

Solve the first level of this dilemma, and the second level will begin to solve itself.

Going Inside

Exactly how does one "go inside" oneself?
—*Marian, 48, Atlanta*

Thank you for an invaluable question. When you know exactly what it means to go inside, many riddles about personal growth begin to clear up. Actually, everyone is already going inside. If someone asks you how you feel or what you think or if you remembered to lock the back door, you automatically go inward for the answer. Your attention is no longer on the outside world but on the inside world.

What do you find when you go inside? A rich world, streaming with thoughts, feelings, sensations, memories, hopes, wishes, dreams, and fears. No one is immune to the allure of this world. We experience ourselves in here, and everything we can possibly imagine. But for every experience that's pleasurable, there's another that is painful.

Here is the starting point of spiritual growth, because human beings, seeing that their pain was centered inside—through painful thoughts, memories, foreboding, and guilt—wanted a way out. Is it possible to go inside and not experience pain? Even when you feel happy and your day is going well, the shadow of bad things to come cannot be denied. So the level of thinking isn't where the cure for pain exists. No one can control painful thoughts.

Therefore, all the great spiritual guides have taught that there is another level of the mind, where silence dominates. If you can experience this silence, your mind begins to shift. Instead of being dominated by fear, guilt, and other forms of inner pain, it is dominated by a quiet, steady state. From this state blossoms a sense of well-being and a feeling that you are safe. If you remain on the path and keep experiencing inner silence, peace dawns, and then joy and bliss. This is the unfoldment of the true self. It's the whole meaning of "going inside."

Teachers and Guides

If someone has a problem finding their purpose in
life, can another person (maybe a spiritual teacher)
do it for them?

—*Irene, 34, Istanbul*

Your question is on the mind of every seeker, whether
they are spiritual or seeking something else, such as love
and success. For many people this process is helped along
by finding a mentor. I've never heard anyone warn, "Be
careful. Don't let your mentor turn you into a mindless
follower." Yet one hears that quite often when it comes to
spiritual seeking.

I mention this because I don't know if you deeply want
a spiritual teacher or, at the other extreme, fear being overly
influenced by a counselor or guide. Let me say that no one
can take from you what you don't willingly give. There
are countless so-called teachers who want to seize power
and control (not just in spirituality but in all walks of
life). You must be careful not to allow this. The best safe-
guard is alertness. Be aware of who you are and what
you seek. You are not here to gratify any teacher, mentor,
or guide. You are here to fulfill your deepest personal
goals.

You can see why your question doesn't lead to a simple
answer. Yes, a guide can help point the way to your own
sense of self and your purpose in life. No, a guide can't replace your own search. When you are in your car driving

through town, signposts can tell you where each road goes, but only you can turn the steering wheel.

Where Do We Come From?

I'm confused. If we all come from the same source, then where does individuality come into play? I believe that we all come from God. We are God living a human life. But I am still struggling with how my individual life could mean anything if we are all the same spirit.

—*Helen, 31, Terre Haute, Indiana*

If I may say so, you've seized on a very abstract dilemma, and now it serves to make you feel insecure. I'd guess that your motive isn't to find a final, absolute answer. If you received a text message from God saying, "I contain all things. The wholeness of creation is expressed through individuality, just as individuality contains and expresses infinite intelligence," would you suddenly feel secure? I'm afraid not.

The issue here isn't where people get their individuality, but how you feel about yourself. Something about who you are is deeply bothering you. Since your letter doesn't give clues to the source of this insecurity, it could be hiding somewhere. Most people look in the mirror and know what they dislike about themselves (I don't mean just physically). At your age, thirty-one, the list of flaws is usually long (it's generally an age when people put heavy demands on themselves, and heavy demands lead to disappointments).

This kind of self-consciousness doesn't mean you are inferior. It means that you are becoming mature and seeing yourself in realistic terms. Having seen that you aren't perfect, you can leave adolescence behind and come to terms with reality. This isn't a curse or a burden. It's not something to avoid. Indeed, finally facing reality is the great adventure of life. Beyond maturity are horizons and paths that lead to the heart of many mysteries. I encourage you to explore them. Perhaps, as you say, God made all of us, but he (or she) didn't have to use a cookie cutter, did he?

Learning to Change

How do you change? At fifty-nine years old, how do you learn to think a new way, see through new eyes, keep growing with the fluidity of youth? How do I keep the curiosity and wonderment of every day alive? Perhaps I've simply lost touch somewhere along the way.

—*Barbara, 59, Eugene, Oregon*

I'm afraid your chief obstacle is your belief system, which you have absorbed from others around you. In this belief system, youth is a time of change and flexibility. Really? In actuality the young are the most insecure among us, and the least able to make mature life choices.

They stumble and experiment. They worry about finding a self.

In another part of the same belief system, to be middle-aged is to be washed up. You think the best of life has passed you by. Instead of renewal and freshness, there's the day-to-day struggle not to fall into boredom and lack of enthusiasm. In actuality, in middle age you know who you are. You have a self. You've arrived.

So the answer to your dilemma is that you must examine your stuck beliefs and old conditioning. Talk with those who aren't burdened by such limiting beliefs. This will require a bit of courage. You feel safe in your gloomy shell. Yet if you look around, you'll see middle-aged people who are enthusiastic, accomplished, ready for any challenge, and eager for tomorrow. Be with them. Be open to what they believe about life. Change will come.

Different Faiths

I converted to Buddhism in 1993, but my family is Christian, and they constantly remind me that I won't be with them in heaven when I die. Usually I just smile and nod because I don't know how to respond. They are always praying for me. What can I do about this constant guilt trip?
—*Mira, 57, Albany, New York*

From what you intimate, your family is very traditional and closely bonded. Be happy for that if you can.

Trying to achieve close bonding is an enormous difficulty in the lives of millions of people. But every good thing is entangled with other things that aren't so good. In traditional societies, religion is what makes you who you are: a member of a family, tribe, ethnic group, race, and culture.

Perhaps only a few of these identity tags apply to your situation, but your letter could just as easily be coming from someone whose family was aghast that she was marrying a man of another skin color or ethnic group. Tradition makes people want to cling to their identity. Change is the enemy.

At fifty-seven, you need to accept their perspective and move on. You are too old to be placating your family. One would expect such worries from a person half your age. I suspect that you are giving them mixed signals. You do everything you can to get your family to believe that you are still the old you, the one they fully accept. Yet an odd difference, Buddhism, sticks out.

You can't change their resistance, but you can stop playing both sides of the fence. Show them that you are happy and secure being a Buddhist. Make clear that criticism isn't fair or welcome. The next time it crops up, leave the room or the house. Keep doing this until they get the message that your deeply held beliefs are off limits. The rest of you is someone they can accept.

The Man Upstairs

For quite some time I've struggled with God always being referred to as "He." Can you suggest how I can be more accepting of this gender bias? Or should I seek a more neutral approach to God, with no gender at all?

—*Doria, 36, Philadelphia*

In the Judeo-Christian tradition, the concept of God as male has become ingrained. It leads millions of people to imagine a patriarch with a long white beard, sitting on a throne above the clouds. I don't know if this irks you, threatens you, arouses a sense of unfairness, or simply strikes you as too limiting for a universal deity who is all-embracing.

In the East believers tend to want it both ways, personal and universal. Personal deities are worshipped and prayed to, with various images and shrines, in the belief that having a humanized object to look at and venerate is only human. At the same time, however, it's understood that the true nature of the Godhead is infinite, beyond limits, and boundless. Two compatible versions of God coexist. Does that work for you?

If not, my best advice is to use this dilemma as part of your spiritual growth. Get to the bottom of what really bothers you. Explore the question with others. Read and grow. One thing I would warn against: don't let this single issue—or any other—become a thorn in your side. There's a lot more to the spiritual path than whether a letter mailed to God should be labeled Mr. or Ms.

A Lonely Seeker

I've been searching for God for several years. I've also been on antidepressants for the biggest part of my life. I have felt the presence of God before, and the feeling was awesome but fleeting. I work as a nurse in hospice, and I can see other people's concept of God comforting them, yet I can no longer connect with a greater consciousness or the traditional God. I believe far more in science and the probability that there is no afterlife. It's a very lonely feeling, but why pray? When I pray I feel like I'm just talking to myself.

I want to find another concept of God that I can hope for. Atheists have nothing to hope for. I know there are no right and wrong answers, yet maybe there's another way to see the meaning of life without a "heavenly father."

—*Cora, 52, Taos, New Mexico*

I've quoted your letter at length because many readers will empathize with you and would put their situation in the same terms. It's much easier to walk out of a church or temple than to find a new one to walk into. There really is no new door, however. There is only a journey. Traditional religion has the advantage of being ready-made. If you pray, follow the commandments, believe in the theology, and don't stray, you have no need to forge your own path.

You are beyond ready-made paths, and despite your loneliness, you should honor yourself for where you've arrived. You aren't at the end of the road, nor are you at the end of belief. This is a way station. There are many steps ahead once you find out how to walk them. Because you work with the dying, you don't have the luxury of avoiding the big questions about life and death that most of us delay until a crisis shakes us out of our inertia. For you, death isn't an idle topic. Much in your life depends on sorting out the relationship between life and death. Instead of turning this into a burden, you could choose to make it an advantage. Appreciate that you are motivated to find out who God really is.

I think for you the best thing would be to solve your lonely feeling first, however. Even though you don't live in a major city, I'm sure that there are spiritual groups nearby where people would welcome you on the terms you offer: you are a troubled seeker who wants new answers. So are they. Find the like-minded, and experience fellowship and support from them. You are a born helper. It's time you helped yourself by nourishing the part of you that wants to belong and be comforted. The God part will come in due course.

Did I Make Myself Sick?

I was diagnosed with breast cancer last February at the age of thirty-eight. Since then I've read a lot about the mind-body connection. Now that my treatments

are finished, I can't escape a nagging doubt: Could
I have caused my cancer through my thought patterns, negative or otherwise? I've read one explanation, which says that breast cancer arises from
nurturing others while ignoring your own needs. Is
this true? I feel so guilty thinking this way.

—*Yasmin, 39, Santa Monica, California*

One of the frustrating things about mind-body medicine is that so many patients, perhaps the majority, focus
on "How did I do this to myself?" Guilt substitutes for
healing. Nagging doubts block the intention to heal. As
this worry turns into an obsession, it gets entangled with
lots of other anxieties, chief among them the fear of recurrence. Thus what started out as help in getting the mind
to aid the body turns on its head, and the mind becomes
a place of dread, worry, and fear.

How do you get out of this vicious circle? What can
release the mind's help without incurring its pain?

First, realize that you have put yourself into a double
bind by blaming the mind. Imagine your mind as your
parent instead. Would it work to say, "I need your love because you're the one who hurt me in the first place?" No,
because once you blend love and hurt, blame and healing,
the two poles war against each other. What you are feeling,
and describing, is inner conflict.

Second, face the conflict. The issue isn't "Did I do this
to myself?" The issue is "What can I do about the war inside myself?" Rest assured, no studies indicate that there
are "cancer personalities." Despite the hypothetical link

between the emotional style of a person and the possibility of being at high risk for disease, such links are very, very far from dooming anyone to cancer. Genetic links are also far from simple. In fact, no one-to-one correlation has been established between anything and breast cancer.

Third, having faced the real problem, consider the positive side of mind-body medicine. It's a vast field, and what it offers is a route to wellness in general. That is a great thing for all of us to bring into our lives. Look at your situation and decide, as realistically as you can, what two things out of the following list would lead to wellness:

- less external stress
- a supportive group of survivors
- treatment for anxiety and depression
- a deeper understanding of the latest mind-body research
- spiritual exploration and growth
- medical reassurance
- a helper to cope with everyday demands
- better working conditions
- meditation to calm your mind
- being touched and soothed physically (massage, bodywork, etc.)
- emotional closeness from a partner
- prevention and lifestyle changes

Your enemy is isolation and the lonely, helpless feeling that it brings. In this list of suggestions, each one helps to combat isolation and helplessness. It's up to you to examine yourself from the inside in order to assess your immediate needs. Modern medicine is impersonal, I regret to say. The support of traditional society is long in the past for most of us. So it falls to each patient to structure his or her own wellness. I encourage you to begin this journey. The dark time you are experiencing now can be healed.

At Peace but Not Happy

Is inner peace the same as happiness? I cannot say that I'm happy, but I'm no longer sure this is even the appropriate question. I do feel an inner peace that appears to be persistent. Would that peace disappear if I found myself homeless or freezing with cold? Would it disappear if I won the lottery? Maybe I need to find ways to stay connected with this peace in extreme circumstances.

—*James, 48, Cork, Ireland*

You aren't experiencing peace. You are caught in stasis, and what most people would call the blahs, you call peace. Sad to say, millions of us are grateful to be blah, because it's a lot better than being homeless or ill. However, even though hiding in a hole is certainly safe, it's nobody's notion of sheer bliss.

Happiness has become a hot topic of research in psychology, and I suspect that you have encountered some of that. One branch of so-called "positive psychology" echoes your belief that happiness is temporary and fleeting.

Outside conditions contribute to whether we feel happy or sad. So does an "emotional set point," which for some people is preset on the sunny side and for others on the gloomy side. Yet whatever makes a person happy or sad, research suggests that personal choice is the biggest factor. Which means that your peace is the result of making choices in the past. We have all been conditioned to mistake ingrained beliefs for reality and stubborn habits for the inevitable.

There are other kinds of choices that bring a new level of happiness, known as bliss or ecstasy. This sort of happiness is permanent, deep, and part of your true self. It's the only happiness that no one can take away from you. Once you have explored the choices open to you, you can decide if you want to settle for your current state of peace. If you decide to move ahead, the path is one of expanded awareness—that's the secret to experiencing happiness and peace at the same time.

Finding Forgiveness

How can I be sure I have completely forgiven my former spouse for his abuse, abandonment, and alcoholism? Can this really be done properly without contacting him? We were together for twenty years, and I haven't spoken to him since the messy divorce fifteen years ago. Through much work spiritually I have learned to embrace all the good things we had together. I feel compassion for him and his abusive childhood. Is this enough? I am more content and confident than ever, but I must have more work to do here.

—*Ellen, 53, Virginia Beach, Virginia*

You are asking a question to which the answer might seem self-evident. What if you had written, "How do I know if my arm doesn't hurt anymore?" When pain is gone, it's gone. But the mind isn't that simple, for two reasons, and both apply here.

First, there's more than one layer of pain in the mind. You are experiencing residual pain that lies deeper than you have yet reached. It's lodged in a place where your identity is. In this place you may not want to remember the past or hold on to it, yet somehow another aspect of yourself says, "I have to hold on."

It's complicated to get at such feelings because in a sense you must unwind a whole tangled ball of yarn, pulling out some threads and keeping others. Intensive self-examination and often long-term psychological therapy are required, with no guarantee of success. In my experience, the deepest trauma turns into one's cross to bear. I'm sorry to use that phrase, but please know that old burdens can be lightened. You have been lightening yours for fifteen years, and the healing process will continue, thanks to your degree of self-awareness.

Second, the mind keeps looking at itself and finding flaws. This is a familiar game and one you can't win. Your letter expresses self-doubt more than residual rage against your husband. Thus in writing to him you hope—in fantasy—to gain his support or an apology. Banish this from your mind; it will never happen. Self-doubt also comes through in your remark that not finding a new relationship reflects something left undone by you.

If so, what's left undone is finding your own feet and becoming your own person without a man. One big reason that you stayed married to an alcoholic husband who abused you was that you desperately believed you needed him. That need continues to linger in the back of your mind, and you hope you can transfer it to a new man in your life. My best advice is to work more on finding your true self and less on forgiveness. Forgiveness will come when being yourself is enough to fulfill you.

A Blessed Soul or Peter Pan?

I've enjoyed my life, and since the age of twenty-two I've always felt blessed with a deeper connection to God. I've come to know that I'm a spiritual being living a human experience. But my career has been very erratic. I've always moved on when a job wasn't fulfilling or another opportunity presented itself. Currently I'm unemployed and on the verge of bankruptcy. Yet deep inside I know that everything is unfolding perfectly and that my children and I will be okay (I've been divorced for fifteen years).

My question is this: Why am I continually at-

SPIRITUAL SOLUTIONS *169*

tracting lack into my life when I'm trying to attract abundance?

—*Teddy, 53, Toledo, Ohio*

Several aspects of your story don't hang together. A connection to God implies self-knowledge, but you seem mystified by how you got where you are today. You call yourself blessed, but you seem rather unconcerned about leading a life that probably has put a good deal of stress on your family. My instinct is that this isn't about attracting lack or abundance. In my experience, two types of men move restlessly from job to job. The first kind are creative, curious, lively people who love new challenges, dislike routine, and keep their eye fixed on the next horizon. The second type are irresponsible, restless, and unable to grow up. They are the Peter Pans of this world, a charming trait when you're a boy, but not so good when you're supposed to be an adult.

So, which are you?

Once you have seriously examined yourself and found the answer, your present situation will become clearer. If you are creative and curious, then probably you need to start your own business and find an outlet that won't turn into a bore in six months or a year. If you are the second type, however, things will continue to be rough. Probably the best you can do is simply find another job from which you will eventually move on. The sad thing is that at fifty-three, your time is running out, and so is your strategy for not turning into a mature person.

FOUR

CREATING YOUR OWN SOLUTIONS

Consciousness leads to solutions by its own nature. Once you know this, your life will require much less struggle. In every situation, if you allow your consciousness to do what it naturally wants to do, the quickest and most creative way to meet any challenge will unfold itself. So what does consciousness want to do? It wants to express itself. That's a very general answer, like saying that a seedling wants to reach the sun or that a child wants to grow up. In living things, self-expression is always present, but to see what is really happening, we have to examine the specifics. At any given moment a seedling is performing numerous processes at the cellular level, and inside a young child's brain millions of neural pathways are maturing.

What are the specifics when it comes to consciousness? The answer can be broken down into the qualities of consciousness. You've already read about the twists and turns of problems to which people want personal answers. Behind these personal difficulties lie broader aspects of how life works, and since life is consciousness in action, nothing is more helpful than standing back and examining the essential qualities of your own awareness. Our examination will be a bit abstract at first; afterward we'll look at how to apply these qualities to our situation here and now.

Once you realize that consciousness is trying to express itself, simply allowing that to happen is enough. You don't have to intervene, plan, calculate, or manipulate your awareness. In fact, this is the first quality of consciousness:

Quality No. 1: Consciousness *works within itself.*

I remember a spiritual teacher being asked, "Is the growth of awareness something we do or something that happens to us?" Without pause he replied, "It feels like something you are doing, but actually it's something that is happening to you. Consciousness is unfolding within itself. You don't drive it. It drives itself." To see the importance of this point, think of consciousness as being like the ocean. Oceans are vast ecosystems that support life; they contain everything needed inside themselves: water, chemicals, food, oxygen, and an array of living things. Each living thing leads its own existence. Corals don't think about fish and vice versa. The balance of nature is such that simply by being itself, fulfilling its own needs, every form of sea life supports every other form. The ocean is self-sufficient. In the same way, consciousness contains everything it needs to regulate your life, leaving nothing out. Cells are within its reach, and so are thoughts. Feel-

ings are overseen by consciousness, and so are muscle reflexes.

In this first quality, many things are implied. First,
there is nowhere else you need to go in order to find a solution. Since it is all-embracing, consciousness contains all
possibilities, which means that the solution you are seeking
already exists in potential. You can trust your own awareness, but your trust doesn't lead to egotism or isolation.
Answers that come from other people, even from totally
unexpected sources, are just as available. Working within
itself, consciousness wants to find the answer at the same
time that you do. You are connected to wholeness.

Quality No. 2: Consciousness uses *intelligent feedback loops.*

It can easily be seen that consciousness is always on the
move, because our minds are a constant stream of thoughts
and sensations. To be alive is to be dynamic. This dynamism isn't random. To sustain life, there has to be purpose.
A cheetah running after a gazelle is no different from an
amoeba going through cell division or a child learning
the first letters of the alphabet. Consciousness is pursuing
a goal. But goals change and they often clash. A cheetah
also needs to sleep; an amoeba needs to seek light; a child
needs to play. In order to balance the myriad functions
that keep you alive, your consciousness talks to itself, sees
what it is doing, and changes course when it needs to.

The technical term for this kind of self-monitoring is

a feedback loop. The classic example of a feedback loop is a thermostat, because it senses when the temperature is too warm or too cold and adjusts the heat accordingly. The example doesn't go nearly far enough to describe a living feedback loop, however. The feedback loops that run your body coordinate hundreds of functions; they respond to changes both "in here" and "out there"; they run automatically but also pay attention to your wishes and intentions; finally, they are intelligent. The ability of consciousness to intelligently monitor brain, body, action, reaction, thoughts, feelings, and intentions is a miracle so vast in scope that no one will ever fully comprehend it. Yet everything you do depends upon it. The best solutions take advantage of as much intelligent feedback as possible.

Quality No. 3: Consciousness seeks balance.

Even if we will never unravel the full mystery of consciousness, we need to understand the basics, and one of these is balance. As it monitors itself, your awareness is making sure that no process runs to extremes without being drawn back. In the body this is known as homeostasis, and it's a peculiar kind of balance. Unlike a mechanical balance scale with two pans that go up and down depending on which side is heavier, the body maintains dynamic balance, meaning that even when everything is on the move, homeostasis isn't thrown off.

Imagine a young runner training for a race who doesn't

know that she's just become pregnant. As she runs, her lungs, heart rate, and blood pressure keep the right balance of nutrients and oxygen, a balance very different from what the body needs at rest. At the same time the hormonal changes associated with pregnancy are automatically kicking in. The brain is controlling both the voluntary side (wanting to go for a run) and the involuntary side (making a baby). At a certain point the woman will register that she doesn't feel the same as usual. The physical signs of pregnancy will come to her awareness, and then she will make new decisions that will lead to a new kind of balance.

Life is much more dynamic than just going for a run and making a baby. Homeostasis regulates hundreds of functions at every moment. But in this example we see the three domains of consciousness: voluntary, involuntary, and self-aware. In other words, to be in balance you do what you want to do, allow the automatic processes to run as they need to, and keep watch on both. A truly effective solution reaches into all three domains and keeps them in balance.

Quality No. 4: Consciousness is endlessly creative.

Even when we grasp that life works through intelligent feedback loops, we haven't yet arrived at the real secret. Feedback loops don't need to evolve. Early life-forms like blue-green algae or one-celled amoebas were tremendous successes. They could have survived forever without evolving, as we see by the fact that they have already flourished unchanged for two billion years. Nothing visible in a cell gives the slightest clue that new life-forms are going to emerge. Indeed, nothing at the instant of the Big Bang implied that stars and galaxies would appear. That first instant was a swirl of superheated matter in its most primitive state, containing subatomic particles in embryo. As matter and antimatter collided, the result was annihilation for both. The universe could have—in fact, should have—collapsed back into the void from which it was born. But it didn't.

Matter exceeded antimatter by around one part in a billion, and that tiny imbalance led to the visible universe, giving rise to DNA on planet Earth eleven billion years later. At the level of consciousness, an infinite thirst for creativity seems to have been at work. We don't need to go into the speculation that the cosmos is alive and always has been. Reduced to personal experience, the drive of creativity is evident everywhere in your life. Since birth, your body has been growing and developing; using its raw potential, you have mastered a set of skills such as reading and writing but also any number that suit your own desires (sailing, walking a tightrope, playing the violin); your brain has confronted a unique stream of data from the outside world, amounting to billions of bits per hour, streaming through the five senses, and every minute is unique, never exactly duplicating that stream from the moment before.

In the midst of this flood of new experience, you have no choice but to be creative. Your cells don't store life. It is estimated that cells retain only a few seconds' or minutes' worth of food and oxygen, which is why the brain can suffer permanent damage with as little as seven to ten minutes of oxygen deprivation. Adapting to all kinds of climate, diet, altitude, humidity, and other variables in the environment requires enormous creativity, and we haven't even arrived at what we normally think of as creative—the work we do, the arts and crafts we pursue, the responses we give to our thoughts, feelings, and desires. Yet from this astonishing complexity one strand runs through everything: consciousness seeks to be as creative as possible. The best solutions allow this inner hunger to be satisfied without restraint.

Quality No. 5: Consciousness absorbs every part into the whole.

If you look around, you see infinite variety in nature. A teaspoonful of dirt from your garden could occupy the entire lifetime of a biologist to understand, and even then he would have to depend on specialists in insects, microorganisms, and chemistry. If something contains infinite parts, what is the whole like? It can't be more than the sum of its parts, because nothing is larger than infinity. The universe isn't more than the sum of its atoms, molecules, stars, and galaxies. The body isn't more than its five trillion cells. Yet somehow consciousness defies such logic.

The infinity of consciousness is bigger than the infinity of its parts. I've saved this concept for last because it is the most abstract; at the same time, it is also the most crucial. Consider the thoughts in your head. A machine could be invented that ticked off each thought like a turn-stile clicking off customers entering a store. Between the cradle and the grave you will tick off a certain number of thoughts, let's say ten million. But how many thoughts are possible in a lifetime? That number is much bigger than ten million. Instead of thinking about the color blue, at any given moment you can think of any color. Instead of buying a Fuji apple at the market this morning, you could have bought any fruit—or nothing at all. In other words, the potential to think is infinite, even though the actual thoughts that come into your head are finite.

The infinite potential of consciousness constitutes its true reality. What we experience isn't even the tip of the iceberg, because icebergs are solid objects. Consciousness contains every possible impulse of the mind, every possible configuration of events, and every possible outcome that those events might lead to. By comparison, the cosmologists who theorize that there may be trillions of other universes lying in dimensions we cannot see or contact—the so-called multiverse theory—have barely considered the scope of reality. There is more than one size of infinity, and consciousness embraces them all.

Let's take a step back from this breathtaking view. As an individual, you take comfort in *not* facing infinity. You don't want countless varieties of apples existing in in-finite grocery stores. (The great marketing secret of Mc-Donald's is that essentially it sells only one thing—a hamburger—to which a few frills can be added, giving the illusion of choice. This secret was powerful enough to launch the world's most successful fast-food chain.) To remain comfortable, we hide from infinity, but in so doing we are hiding from reality. There is a "reality illusion" that denies the infinite nature of consciousness. We all live in our own bubble, taking ourselves to be the center of the world—that's where the reality illusion is manufactured and upheld, moment by moment.

If you sit in a restaurant and look around, it's not hard to see how each person constructs their own reality illusion. One person is withdrawn, another outgoing. One feels victimized and defensive, another in control and expansive. Each person builds boundaries from basic materials like success and failure, belonging or being an outsider, playing the victim or the martyr, the boss or the underling, leader or follower. In order to find a solution that works, you must dismantle your own reality illusion in order to arrive at the *real* reality, which is consciousness. The five qualities we've just covered offer an opening to becoming real, and that is enough to solve any problem. Solutions are always available at the level of reality; problems arise at the level of the reality illusion.

BREAKING DOWN THE ILLUSION

Now we have the mechanics for any spiritual solution: let your inner awareness express itself. The technique couldn't be simpler. You stop interfering with what your higher consciousness wants to do. It takes a shift in perspective to begin to implement this strategy, because everyone is used to jumping into situations with prefabricated responses. Those who rely on control try to control the situation. Those who compete try to win and be number one. Those who can't stand confrontation lie back and hope that "things will work out." It may seem at first glance that this last option is the one I am advocating. Are you supposed to stand aside and let consciousness do whatever it wants, like watching a seed grow after you've watered it?

In a way, yes. But there's a big difference. You can't stand aside from consciousness. You need to let it unfold without resisting, yet at the same time you give your full participation. There's no other choice, since even the most passive, aloof, or uninvolved person has made a choice to be that way; they are participating in doing nothing. I'm not recommending passivity. There is a lot to do when you want a solution that comes from the deepest level of awareness.

HOW TO AWAKEN YOUR DEEP AWARENESS

Look at your hidden assumptions and beliefs.

Remove the obstacles you're raising. Stop resisting.

Become objective.

Take responsibility for your own feelings. Don't blame or project.

Ask for answers to come from every direction.

Trust that the solution is there, waiting to unfold.

Become part of the discovery. Use curiosity. Follow hunches and intuition.

Be willing to turn on a dime. Quick changes are part of the discovery process.

Accept that everyone inhabits his or her own reality bubble. Become aware of the reality that other people are coming from.

Approach every day as if it's a new world, because it is.

Until you follow these steps, the possibility of finding new answers will be very limited, because you are reinforcing your reality illusion when what is needed is a breakout. It takes energy to maintain an illusion; you have to be constantly vigilant to defend your boundaries; you censor the messages coming into your awareness that you don't like and favor those that fit your concept of what is acceptable. In short, the reality illusion is a construct for creating problems. It isn't a construct for creating solutions.

If this checklist seems too daunting, let me share a simple technique that works for me. In any given situation, I don't act until I run through the ingrained, unconscious things that my first impulse tells me to do. The choices are not many. You can choose from a short menu of very basic options:

Emotionally, I react to negative situations by being
    angry
    anxious

When action is called for, I am usually
  leading
  following
If someone else is doing something I don't like,
I usually
  confront
  withdraw
Given a major challenge, I prefer to
  be part of a group
  go it alone
If I sit back to view myself overall, my style is
  dependent: I let others make the big decisions. I
  like being liked. I put off tough decisions. I often
  don't say what I feel, or do what I really want to do.
  controlling: I am fussy about details. I have
  standards and expect others to live up to them.
  I've been called a perfectionist. I find it easy to
  tell others what to do. I find excuses for my bad
  decisions but hold grudges against others.
  competitive: I am always aware of who is winning
  and losing. I go the extra mile to be on top. I see
  myself as a leader and others as followers. I like to
  perform and often feel that I have to. I find it
  easy to step over other people, but I also crave the
  approval of others.

In any situation, I keep in mind how I will reflexively
react, and I take a moment to stop doing what comes
automatically. By stepping back, I ask for a different, more

flexible response to emerge, either inside me or in my surroundings. This isn't the same as making myself wrong. Instead, I allow expanded awareness to have a chance. Unless it is given a chance, the only response available to me will be the same anger or anxiety, leading or following, winning or losing. Life is ever fresh. It cannot be met with conditioned responses. If life is to renew itself, you must renew your reactions as well.

SEVEN LEVELS OF ILLUSION

By breaking down your own reality illusion—the one that is unique to you—you accomplish two things: first, you come out of contracted awareness into expanded awareness; second, you merge into the intelligent feedback loops that are in charge of every aspect of life. Naturally, the process needs to be more specific, so let me outline seven levels of problems that arise from contracted awareness and the solutions that take you one step closer to reality.

Level 1: Problems created by fear, anger, and other negative impulses

The basic response is defensive. Anger and fear are primal but unevolved. Almost all your energy is directed at survival. At this level you want to lash out and blame others. You feel frustrated that the situation is happening.

Everything seems to be out of control, and as others put more pressure on you—or even direct abuse at you—you contract with anxiety and anger.

You are stuck at this level if you feel helpless, victimized, anxious, paralyzed, lost, or in need of guidance from those who are stronger than you. Weakness dominates your response.

The solution: Feel your negative response, but don't trust it. Move beyond fear and anger. Ask for guidance from people who aren't reacting at such a primal level. Make no decisions until you feel balanced and clear once more. Haste is your enemy. Impulse control is your ally.

Level 2: Problems created by your ego

The basic response is self-centered. Thoughts arise like "This shouldn't be happening to me. I don't deserve it," or "Nobody is doing what I want." At this level you don't feel afraid; you feel blocked in getting what you want, usually because someone else's ego is opposing yours. A spouse doesn't agree with your way of doing things; a boss has ideas about how to get things done that are different from your ideas; you see the goal but can't reach it despite your drive to win and accomplish.

You are stuck at this level if you feel overly competitive, contrarian, driven, blocked by opponents, unsuccessful, or like a loser. "What about me?" dominates your thinking.

The solution: Start to share and give, especially of yourself. Let others stand in the limelight with you. Pass around the credit for achievements; take responsibility for setbacks. Stop focusing on external rewards like money and status. Make others feel equal to you. Perceiving every situation as win or lose is your enemy. Finding inner fulfillment is your ally.

Level 3: Problems created by conformity

The basic response is going along to get along. You want to fit in and not make waves, but peer pressure is making you give away too much. You feel that certain core values, such as self-respect and honesty, or worthiness and independence, have been sacrificed. Thoughts arise like "This isn't me," or "I don't agree with what everyone else is saying." You get into binds that involve making promises you can't keep, pretending to be more competent than you really are, or even faking it in order to fit in.

You are stuck at this level if you feel anonymous, untrue to yourself, passive, bullied, coerced, lost in the shuffle, or empty. Dull conformity dominates your thinking, and probably a not-so-secret urge to rebel.

The solution: Take back the power you gave away. Speak your truth when it counts. Draw a line when your core values are violated. Stay out of cliques and factions. Walk away from gossip. Learn to question conventional wisdom and group-think. Give a higher priority to self-respect. Falling into line is your enemy. Becoming an individual is your ally.

Level 4: Problems created by not being understood and appreciated

The basic response is to isolate yourself. Because you don't feel that others understand you, you retreat inside, becoming lonely and unsupported by people around you. It becomes difficult either to love or be loved. Personal connections fray; there is little ability to bond. You wonder if you even matter.

You are stuck at this level if you feel alone, abandoned, unloved, unappreciated, shut out, shut down, or drifting. "Nobody is here for me" dominates your thinking.

The solution: Seek the company of mature people who are capable of empathy. Examine how you isolate yourself through silence, walking away, and passivity. Show that you value your feelings by actually expressing them. Show the same understanding that you want to receive. Wearing a mask is your enemy, even a pleasant mask. Opening up our inner world is your ally.

Level 5: Problems created by being unique

The basic response is self-expression without limits. You want to be the most you can be, and this drive has led you into art, discovery, invention, and other outlets for creativity. What others call your narcissism is what you call your inspiration. You are frustrated unless life brings something new every day; you crave being recognized. This attitude, which should be liberating, leads to problems in meeting the needs of others. Authority rankles and makes you want to break free. Rigid rules were created for other people, not you.

You are stuck at this level if you feel stifled in your creativity, blocked by the stupidity or conformity of others, answerable only to your own muse, or entitled to be yourself no matter what the cost. "I have to be me" dominates your thinking, and you feel justified by your uniqueness.

The solution: Form attachments to other creative types. Allow relationships to anchor you, so that you are more in touch with reality. Treasure fantasy, but don't get lost in it. Share your talents by teaching and giving of your time. Be a mentor. Look to greater minds for inspiration and also humility. Vanity is your enemy. Constantly renewing your imagination is your ally.

Level 6: Problems created by being a visionary

The basic response is idealism. You possess a strong moral compass. Thinking little about yourself, you want to improve the human condition. But your lofty vision, as much as it inspires some people, brings up resistance in others.

They feel as if you are making them wrong, even though that is far from your intention. You want a better existence for everyone, with injustice banished and spiritual equality the norm. You have gone beyond rigid definitions of right and wrong, only to find that countless people follow such definitions and are not open to having them challenged.

You are stuck at this level (a very high one) if you feel weighed down by life's sorrows, disappointed in humanity, overwhelmed by the troubles you see all around you, and baffled by the lack of vision that you meet every day. "I am here to bring the light" dominates your thinking.

The solution: Exercise tolerance. Use moral values to uplift others rather than judge them. Don't try to imitate impossible models, the great sages and saints of the past. Take time for basic enjoyments like laughter and the beauty of nature. Being loved for your perfection is your enemy. Being loved as a person, however fallible, is your ally.

Level 7: The state of no problems

The basic response is openness, acceptance, and peace. You are no longer troubled by a divided self. For you, reality doesn't present itself as good versus evil, light versus darkness, or "me" against "the other." You express the wholeness of life, which is like a river flowing free. You allow the river to move instead of clinging to the banks.

Life unfolds as it was meant to, as if every event, no matter how small, has its place in the divine plan.

You have attained the state of no problems if you feel spontaneously creative, completely at home in the cosmos, eternally at peace, and merged with all of creation. "I am everything" dominates your thinking, although there is no reason to have such thoughts, since unity has become your natural way of being.

FINDING YOUR TRUE SELF

Any good psychologist, even an amateur one who has studied human nature, would agree with the list just given. I think they would also agree that the vast majority of problems occur at the lower levels, where negative impulses and ego are dominant. Much of humanity struggles to survive, and when life becomes easier, the door is opened for the ego's "all about me" thinking. This makes it hard to see how spirituality can make a dent, much less be the guiding light of one's life. The way that spirituality works, however, is not from the bottom up. Fighting to survive is about limitations, which is the state where your true self, or the soul, is most masked and hidden from view.

The world has needed its great spiritual teachers to guide us away from the surface of life. We need to be taught not to believe in the mask that reality wears. As a basic fact, everyone believes in his or her reality illusion.

Despite this fact, however, the *real* reality is untouched by sorrow and struggle. Whether we know it or not, all of us are in the world but not of it. In practical terms, spirituality works from the top down. Your true self is your source. You cannot be separated from it, and therefore you have a choice. Either you move toward the true self, the level of the soul, or you move away from it. One direction is evolutionary; the other is static at best, and usually destructive.

To keep evolving, it is necessary to know the signs of evolution. They indicate that you are getting closer to your true self. To evolve is a process. It has its ups and downs. There are days when you lose sight of it, and others when you stop believing that you are evolving at all. No one is immune from the twists and turns of the spiritual path. Yet the world's great teachers have seen and lived the true self. From them we receive a picture of what pure awareness is, the basis of the true self. With that in mind, it is much easier to measure your own evolution. Here are the most important teachings about the true self, which will then be described in detail. All have practical implications. Working from the top down, the true self is trying to draw closer every day.

WHEN YOU ARE YOUR TRUE SELF

1. Your life has a unique purpose.
2. That purpose is unfolding continually, becoming richer and deeper.

3. If you align yourself with your purpose, that is enough.
4. As your life unfolds, awareness expands without limits.
5. With expanded awareness, desires can be fulfilled completely.
6. Challenges are solved by rising to a level higher than the challenge.
7. Your life is part of a single human destiny: arriving at unity consciousness.

As you can see, nothing here is couched in religious terms. You can rephrase every item using words like *God*, *soul*, or *spirit*, but it's not required. Instead of saying, "My life has a unique purpose," you could say, "God has given my life a unique purpose." The same reality holds even if the terminology changes. Let me expand on each aspect of the true self, with the aim of making them personal to your life here and now.

1. Your life has a unique purpose.

Everyone pursues a purpose in life. The human mind is goal-oriented, and each day brings new desires to fulfill. With a family to raise, relationships to nurture, things to acquire, and a career to focus on, short-term purpose is supplied almost automatically (and when someone loses their sense of purpose, we worry that they are seriously depressed). There is no need to introduce spirituality until you change the question from "Does your life have a purpose?" to "Does life have a purpose?" The second question is much more uncertain. It opens up a gap that needs to be closed. In the world's wisdom traditions, life has always been seen to have a purpose, which can be stated in various ways. *The purpose of life is*

to find out who you really are
to grow and evolve
to reach higher states of consciousness
to experience the divine
to become enlightened

If you can find fulfillment on any of these levels, you are achieving your vision, not simply meeting the demands of everyday existence. A greater vision closes the gap between you and the universe. If life itself has a purpose, your existence fits into the cosmic scheme. The threat that existence is meaningless, which would lead to anxiety and despair, or an aching sense of loneliness, is removed when you are certain of your place in creation.

2. *That purpose is unfolding continually, becoming richer and deeper.*

This principle is about connecting the present and the future. The purpose of life cannot be postponed; unless it unfolds every day, the future will never be anything more than a repetition of old patterns and behavior. Psychologists observe that when old age is a time of satisfaction, looking back on a life well lived, the reason is that the person has successfully met many challenges over the years. For those who find old age empty or bitter, the opposite has happened: relationships didn't work out, careers fell short, families drifted apart. In other words, every day has long-term consequences.

It helps tremendously to know that you are part of a larger scheme. This was once a given—in an age of faith, people lived for the glory of God or to attain salvation. Every day brought you one step closer to your goal. The need for a vision hasn't gone away, but it isn't a given anymore, except for those who retain deep religious faith.

When the purpose of life isn't a given, what is it? A process. You discover the goal of existence by living it. The present is the only time when you can evolve, experience the divine, expand your awareness, or reach enlightenment. But this cannot be a haphazard journey that falters and wanders off the path. It's easy for that to happen when a crisis develops. Sudden losses and setbacks shake everyone up; those who keep moving forward are buoyed by knowing that their path cannot be destroyed, only interrupted.

3. If you align yourself with your purpose, that is enough.

This principle is about effort and struggle. It says that in spirituality, neither is necessary. The cosmic purpose unfolds automatically, not because there is a fixed design, but because creativity and intelligence are built into creation. Nature isn't outside us; it moves in, around, and through us. If you align yourself with the movement of creation, you will experience flow and ease. If you oppose the movement of creation, you will meet obstacles and resistance.

In many ways this is the "crunch point" of everyone's life. If you approach spirituality as an ideal that would be nice to achieve, your real allegiance lies elsewhere. For people ruled by ambition, nothing is more real than getting ahead. For people ruled by anxiety, nothing is more real than the threats they try to keep at bay. Your life at this moment is expressing where your allegiance lies. It could be an allegiance to family, status, money, possessions, career—anything is possible. None of these are bad; they are not unspiritual, in fact. The problem is that such allegiances are superficial, acting out on the surface of life, without the support of spirit, God, the universe— choose whatever term you feel comfortable with.

This means that spirituality becomes practical only when you switch your allegiance to a deeper level. It's not more faith that people need, but more proof, day in and day out, that relying on life's deeper purpose actually works. That's where the process comes in. You move from a fragile beginning, where you hope and wish that God or the universe will support you. Then you reach the middle of the journey, when you have a strong belief that you are supported. Finally you arrive at the place where you know that you are supported. You can move from hope to belief to knowing. It's the natural unfolding of each life, and the journey doesn't take years and years. Every day can bring the fulfillment of hopes and wishes, changing them into certainty that you are seen, understood, and nurtured.

4. As your life unfolds, awareness expands without limits.

This principle tells you where your support will come from. It comes from your own awareness. In order for the process of unfolding to continue, it must grow inside. On the outside, life brings new challenges, and what makes them new is that old answers don't work to solve them. Today's riddles need today's answers. This back-and-forth allows your life to rise continually, because at the deepest level you are inviting the challenges to become more difficult— with greater mysteries come greater revelations.

In an age of faith, God showed his pleasure and displeasure in countless ways. Each believer monitored whether the deity was favoring them or not. Sickness, poverty, and misfortune were signs that God had turned his face away from you. Riches, happiness, and sunny days indicated that God's light shone upon you. But since no one's existence can be either one or the other, the deity seemed fickle and elusive. All manner of theories tried to explain why life brought a mixture of pleasure and pain, but one thing was lacking: a steady assurance that human beings were favored in the universe.

Spirituality is broader than any single religion. While one faith grappled with sin and another with karma, the wider wisdom didn't look to God or any outside power. It looked inward, to consciousness. The fact that life has answers built into it gives us a clue to why Jesus emphasized living in the present: "Therefore do not worry about tomorrow, for tomorrow will worry about itself. Each day has enough trouble of its own" (Matthew 6:34). So that his listeners wouldn't get stuck on the word "trouble," Jesus had another teaching about how troubles are to be met, quoted in Matthew 6:22: "Look at the birds of the air; they do not sow or reap or store away in barns, and yet your heavenly Father feeds them. Are you not much more valuable than they?" In Buddhism the same teaching is given more metaphysically: every question answers itself. So by going within, the very existence of a problem means that its solution exists.

5. With expanded awareness, desires can be fulfilled completely.

This principle tells us that spirituality brings more fulfillment, not less. The path unfolds through the expansion of life, which must follow once awareness expands. The two go together. You see more possibilities; you have less fear; when you act, your actions succeed, and thus success breeds success. All of that can sound quite foreign to traditional religious belief, where renunciation and temptations of the flesh sound much more familiar. The conflict between worldly life and spiritual life was a given for centuries.

Everything depends on how you view your desires. If you see them as selfish, wrong, or sinful, then it's only natural that God would disapprove, too. What happens isn't a punishment delivered by the hand of God; rather, you cut off channels of fulfillment. Desires that are judged against cause inner conflict—you want them to come true, but at the same time you don't. When people say, "I have to fight the urge," they are expressing this conflict. The notion that God, the soul, or the universe supports inner conflict is a drastic mistake. Conflict grows out of itself. As long as you are fighting a war with your own desires, every day brings hope of winning the war and resignation over losing it.

If spirituality is about fulfilling your desires, however, new channels open up. There is a clear connection between wanting and receiving. I realize that many people will instantly object, "But what about bad desires? Are you saying that they don't exist?" We all know that some desires, no matter how we label them, either work out beneficially or lead to setbacks and failure. The terms of morality don't fly out the window when you follow spiritual principles. You develop a finer sense of what is good and what isn't. Good can be defined as being aligned with your spiritual purpose, so that your actions are life-enhancing. Your desires are woven into your evolution. When that happens—and it happens more and more as the process unfolds—then desire becomes the path. This only makes sense, because you can't evolve without wanting to, and a want is the same as a desire. The path that is the most successful in life is guided by desire.

6. Challenges are solved by rising to a level higher than the challenge.

This principle reminds us of the main point in this book: the level of the problem is never the level of the solution. When two parties are fighting, they turn to a judge, because impartiality and detachment are a higher level of awareness than combativeness and a refusal to budge. When a woman is struggling with issues of body image, telling her "You look fine," or "How you look isn't so important," won't help her; the solution is for her to find better ways to feel worthy. When you value yourself for your ability to love, empathize, and be compassionate, it's much harder to be obsessed by what you see in the mirror.

Spiritually, there is a level that is the highest of all. This is the level of transcendence. When you transcend, you release personal attachments. No longer stuck in old habits and conditioning, you ask for your highest awareness to enter the situation and find a solution. Transcending is more than simply letting go. In practical terms, several other steps are involved: You step back from the problem and acknowledge that there is more than one way to look at it. You give up your claim to know the truth already. You open yourself to new possibilities. You remove inner resistance to finding an answer; such resistance might come in the form of anger, resentment, envy, stubbornness, or insecurity. Finally, you invite the answer to unfold any way that it wants to, which means being alert to unexpected shifts and changes—your bitterest opponent may suddenly agree with you, or long-held grievances may melt away.

What makes transcendence viable isn't blind faith. You are allowing a complete worldview to unfold through you. If you don't feel that the earlier principles are true, your higher self won't sweep down on a magic carpet to solve your problems. But if you have dedicated yourself to the process of personal growth and the expansion of consciousness, then powers that once were hidden or blocked will emerge. A famous quotation from the great German writer Goethe proclaims, "Be bold, and mighty forces will come to your aid." Boldness is the ability to step outside boundaries created by fear and insecurity. In other words, you transcend your own limitations. No test of courage is required. As we will discuss, solving problems by rising to a level higher than the problem is one of the most practical and natural ways to achieve success in difficult situations.

7. Your life is part of a single human destiny: arriving at unity consciousness.

This principle tells us about the underlying harmony of life. On the surface, differences predominate. Each of us is proud to be unique and different. The cause of discord can be traced to the same factor, however. If "they" are different from "us," we have an automatic reason to feel estranged and perhaps even hostile to "them." The wars and violent conflicts that never seem to cease are rooted in differences that led to irreconcilable hatred. But at a deeper level, spirituality holds that the clash of opposites— not just "us" versus "them" but also good versus evil, light versus darkness, my God versus your God—can be overcome.

To find the harmony that lies deeper than differences is the primary goal of spirituality. This is not a passive project, fueled by curiosity. Unity is the purest state of awareness. As the eminent physicist Erwin Schrödinger asserted, "Consciousness is a singular that has no plural." There is only one consciousness that you and I express in our unique ways. Our source lies inside each of us, and the goal of every life, no matter how different it looks on the surface from every other, is to reach the source. At that point there are no more divisions, inner or outer. The state of unity has been reached.

I realize that this may sound impossibly high-flown. If you are worried about the mortgage or who your teenage daughter is dating or the threat of extremism in the world, unity consciousness seems to have zero relevance. But nothing could be more relevant, because every spiritual solution comes to us from the level of unity. Things we call inspired, insightful, creative, intuitive, or revelatory are messages from the source. In past ages the vocabulary of religion held a virtual monopoly on how to think about unity consciousness; without God, the soul, or divine grace, there was no viable way to conceive of it.

Which is why this book has been about practical solutions instead. Making the true self relevant to your life, here and now, is the only way that it can come alive. Outside the context of religion, every experience happens in consciousness. If there is a reality beyond the human mind, we will never discover it, since nothing is real until it enters our awareness. If the divine exists but has no contact with human beings, there is no basis for worship and faith. Even though we no longer live in an age of faith, the divine can still be experienced. To meet God isn't like meeting another person, however exalted and awe-inspiring. To experience the divine is to experience the entire domain of higher consciousness, which is infinite. All of it is accessible. I am not asking for a leap of faith. There is no need to journey anywhere mystical. The only necessity is to open yourself to a worldview that begins with your true self as the answer to the challenges that life brings. Since everyone faces such challenges, there is ample motivation to see if better solutions can be found.

If anyone asks, "What is the spiritual solution?" in their particular situation, the best answer is "Seek for one, and you will know." When the toughest problems meet the right answers, there is a deep meeting of the self with the self. This book was written to make that meeting possible.

THE ESSENCE

Consciousness is designed to lead to solutions. All that is needed is to let it unfold naturally and spontaneously. The process is not passive. You must participate in unblocking the flow of your own awareness.

The main block is the "reality illusion" that traps you in limitations. We all believe in our reality illusion. We are uncomfortable with infinity and its endless possibilities. By breaking down the reality illusion, you automatically expand your awareness and life becomes much less of a struggle.

The great secret that illusion hides from us is that we are always connected to the true self, which exists at the level of the soul. The true self drives personal evolution. It sends messages through intuition, insight, and imagination. It arranges the best possible outcome for any situation. The closer you come to the true self, the more you can rely completely on consciousness.

Acknowledgments

Before I ever wrote my own books, I used to turn immediately to the acknowledgments in every book I picked up. I was curious about the web of connections that invisibly tie a book together. Now, as the years of writing pile up, I feel how much such connections really mean. And so my thanks go out first to the editorial and publicity staff that has made this book grow from a seedlike possibility to a reality. Julia Pastore, Tina Constable, and Tara Gilbride gracefully head the list. I would also like to thank Maya Mavjee and Kira Walton.

On a day-to-day basis I couldn't do without the support and affectionate loyalty of Carolyn, Felicia, and Tori. Always in the background but at the front of my heart is my family. Thanks to all.

ABOUT THE AUTHOR

DEEPAK CHOPRA is the author of more than sixty books translated into over eighty-five languages, including numerous *New York Times* bestsellers in both the fiction and nonfiction categories.

www.DeepakChopra.com